WOMEN IN REVOLUTIONARY RUSSIA

CATHY PORTER

ЕЖЕНЕДѢЛЬНЫЙ ЖУРНАЛЪ

1917г. "РАБОТНИЦА" 1917г.

Органъ Центральнаго Комитета.

А. М. КОЛЛОНТАЙ   А. Н. СТАЛЬ

CAMBRIDGE UNIVERSITY PRESS

Cambridge

London   New York   New Rochelle

Melbourne   Sydney

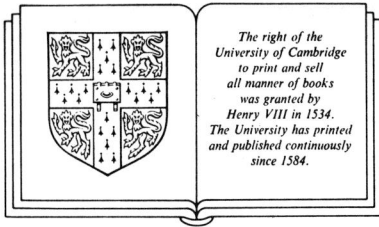

The right of the
University of Cambridge
to print and sell
all manner of books
was granted by
Henry VIII in 1534.
The University has printed
and published continuously
since 1584.

Published by the Press Syndicate of the University of Cambridge
The Pitt Building, Trumpington Street, Cambridge CB2 1RP
32 East 57th Street, New York, NY 10022, USA
10 Stamford Road, Oakleigh, Melbourne 3166, Australia

First published 1987

Printed in Great Britain at the University Press, Cambridge

British Library cataloguing in publication data
Porter, Cathy
Women in revolutionary Russia.
1. Women in politics – Soviet Union – History – 20th
century.   2. Soviet Union – Politics and
government – 1894–1917.   3. Soviet Union – Politics and
government – 1917–1936.   I. Title
947.08′3   DK246

Library of Congress cataloguing in publication data
Porter, Cathy
   Women in revolutionary Russia.
   Bibliography: p. 48
   1. Women in politics – Soviet Union – History – 20th
century.   2. Women revolutionists – Soviet Union –
History – 20th century.   3. Soviet Union – Politics and
government – 1894–1917.   I. Title.
HQ1391.S69P67   1987   305.4′0947   85 – 30954

ISBN 0 521 31969 2

Acknowledgements

The author and publisher would like to thank the following for
permission to reproduce illustrations:

BBC Hulton Picture Library, pp. 9 (bottom), 13, 27

David King Collection, title page, pp. 5 (right), 6 (top and
centre), 7, 16, 17, 19, 20, 28, 30, 34, 39, 40, 43

Mansell Collection, pp. 5 (left), 8 (top and bottom), 37

Novosti Press Agency, pp. 6 (bottom), 11, 14, 44

Society for Cultural Relations with the USSR, pp. 9 (top), 10,
12, 22, 31, 32, 33, 35, 41, 45

Every effort has been made to reach copyright holders; the
publishers would be glad to hear from anyone whose rights they
have unknowingly infringed.

Front cover illustration: adapted from a 1920s poster: peasant
woman with newspapers, including *Working Woman and Peasant
Woman*. War and revolution created a new kind of woman,
strong and independent

Title page: Editors of *Rabotnitsa*, 'Working Woman', *1917*

Author's note

This book does not claim to be a complete picture
of women's lives during the revolutionary period; it
is about women active in the revolutionary
movement, and particularly, in the later period,
those active in the Bolshevik party. To examine
what the revolution meant for women of different
classes and in different organisations would have
made a truly interesting book, but lies outside the
scope of this one, which is a more straightforward
account of the changes that revolution brought to
the women most directly involved in it. Because of
these limitations, the book will naturally be used in
conjunction with other accounts of the revolution.
It is because other accounts deal more fully with
important events of revolutionary history (such as
the Bolshevik–Menshevik split), that I have given
some of these events limited attention.

Contents

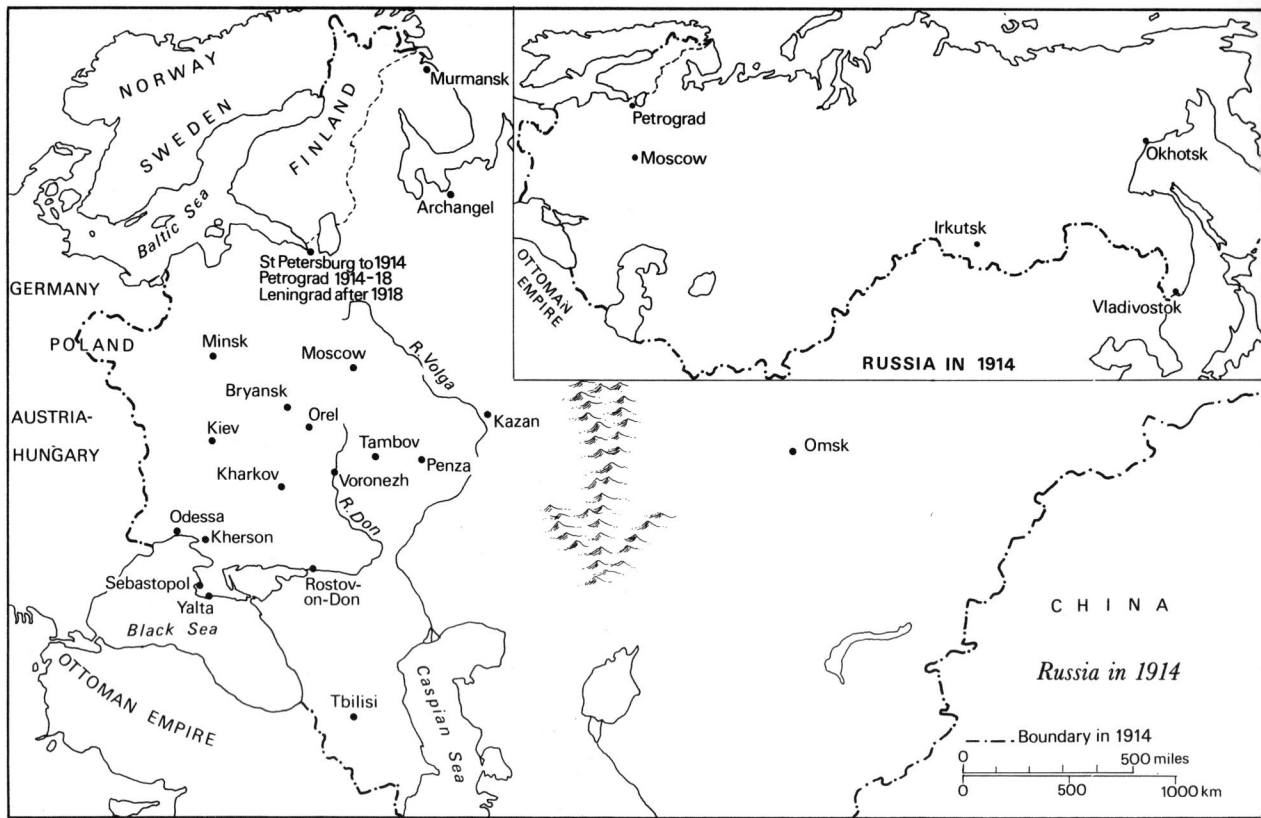

Russia in 1914

RUSSIA IN 1914

--- Boundary in 1914

Key dates

1854–6	Crimean War
1855	Accession of Alexander II; administrative reforms set in motion
1861	Emancipation of the serfs
1862–3	Formation of first Land and Liberty party
1864	Marx's International Workingman's Association (First International) founded in London
1869	After much petitioning by women, first women's courses open in St Petersburg and Moscow
1870	First factory strikes, in St Petersburg
1877–8	First great public show trials in Russia of revolutionaries: 'Trial of Moscow Women' and 'Trial of the 193'
1878	Vera Zasulich's assassination attempt on Governor-General of St Petersburg. Terrorism comes into revolutionary movement
1879	First university courses opened for women, Bestuzhev Courses. Land and Liberty party re-forms as the terrorist People's Will.
1881	March – People's Will members assassinate Tsar Alexander II. Five hanged
1889	Second International founded in Paris, uniting all socialist parties of Europe
1895	Marxist groups in St Petersburg united by Lenin into Union of Struggle for the Emancipation of the Working Class
1896	Huge textile-workers' strike in St Petersburg
1898	Russian Social Democratic Labour Party (RSDRP) founded in Minsk from members of the Union of Struggle for the Emancipation of the Working Class
1901	Formation of Socialist Revolutionary Party, heir to Land and Liberty and People's Will
1902	Publication of Lenin's *What is to be Done?*, on the need for a disciplined revolutionary party
1903	Second Congress of RSDRP, at which split appears between Bolsheviks and Mensheviks
1904	Russia declares war on Japan. Strikes and demonstrations follow
1905	January – 'Bloody Sunday', when hundreds of peaceful demonstrators are killed, is followed by riots, strikes and demonstrations which trigger the revolution. Treaty of Portsmouth ends Russo-Japanese War. By the end of the year, the revolution has been suppressed; years of reaction follow
1913	Women in Russia celebrate for the first time the new women's International Women's Day with protest demonstrations
1914	8 March – International Women's Day (March 8) sees publication of Bolshevik women's paper, *Rabotnitsa*. 4 August – England declares war on Germany: beginning of First World War
1915	Women's 'food riots'. Russia's defeat beyond question
1917	Women's Day is start of revolution, in which Tsar Nicholas II is overthrown, and a new 'Provisional Government' takes power. 24–5 October – Bolsheviks overthrow 'Provisional Government' and take power
1918–20	Russia convulsed by civil war and Western powers' wars of Intervention
1918	November – First All-Russian Congress of Peasant and Working Women; Women's Commissions of the party set up
1919	September – Women's Commissions upgraded to central Women's Department (Zhenotdel), which works to remove the causes of prostitution, to improve maternity services and working conditions for women, to legalise abortions, and to help children orphaned by war and revolution

Russia of the Tsars and Russia of the revolutionaries

1 Since the sixteenth century Russian society had been divided between the **serfs** (see glossary of terms page 46) and the free (the landowners) and ruled over by a **Tsar**. In the Middle Ages the Tsars had been all-powerful and were believed by their subjects to be of divine origin. In the nineteenth century too, the distance between the Tsar and his people was enormous, and in many ways Russia was still a 'medieval' country: there was almost no industry, and most people were illiterate, superstitious and ignorant. But increasing numbers of people now were demanding an end to the hardship and inequality of their lives. The Russian army's defeat in the Crimean War (1854–6), during which soldiers had had to endure appalling conditions and cope with inadequate equipment, was the last straw. Alexander II came to the throne in 1855, as peasants rioted up and down the country. By 1861 the universities had also become the scene for large demonstrations.

Alexander was determined to avert revolution by granting reforms – including the **emancipation** of the serfs in 1861. But his reforms came too late and were not enough. The Russian people had suffered for too long. More and more of them lost hope in the possibility of reform and became revolutionaries, and ultimately terrorists. In 1881 Alexander II was assassinated. His successors, Alexander III and Nicholas II, were keen to rule Russia according to the old tsarist precepts of **autocracy, nationalism** and **religious orthodoxy**.

2 After the emancipation, the peasants continued to live in desperate poverty, paying a variety of crippling taxes to the landlords and the state. The peasant woman's life was doubly hard. Often mistreated by her parents, her husband and her in-laws, exhausted by endless pregnancies and work in the fields, she was regarded as barely human, and her labour was considered 'unproductive'.

'A hen is not a bird and a woman is not a person.' 'I thought I saw two people walking along, but one was a woman.' *Peasant sayings*

Alexander II, Tsar of Russia, 1855–81

Peasant women and children, late nineteenth century

3 In Russia, few landowners lived in style. A small minority were educated but still quite poor, and the great majority lived not much better than the peasants. Women of this class were also often subjected to brutal, drunken husbands and a life of endless childbearing.

Women in Russia have virtually no social significance…People value them neither as wives nor mothers, since until now men have had complete power over them. If a wife decides to change her position in the family and insist on her rights as a wife, you can safely assume that nine out of ten people will condemn her.
E. A. Slovtsova-Kamskaya, a teacher from Perm, in 1860

Nevertheless, in one important way these women were more independent than women in the west, as they kept their right to property (including serfs) after marriage, and many ran estates while their husbands were in town.

4 It was the **Russian Orthodox Church** that gave the Tsar the moral authority to rule. The teachings of the Church reinforced the low regard for women throughout Russian society. It made divorce almost impossible, associated women with numerous vices and sins, and encouraged the image of husbands and fathers as agents of imperial and religious authority. Yet the Church's ideals of self-sacrifice and martyrdom did provide inspiration and strength for many women who later became revolutionaries.

5 The emancipation of the serfs in 1861 left most peasants as badly off as before, and bankrupted many poorer aristocratic families. For many women though, peasant and aristocratic, it spelt liberation. Throughout the 1860s and 70s, thousands of women left the provinces for the towns, particularly for the capital St Petersburg. There, despite public persecution and police harassment, they struggled to live on their own terms. They demanded the right to an education and set up self-education groups. They competed with men for jobs and organised work collectives. They lived intensely, usually communally, and often in great poverty. For them the question of women's rights was central to their lives.

This unique climate saw the rise of the intelligentsia, committed to social and political reform, with women playing an important part

Russian landowners

Russian Orthodox priests

Emancipation is proclaimed to the serfs on the Prozorov Estate in the province of Moscow, 1861

in the growth of this new hybrid 'class'. Many cropped their hair, dressed like peasants and walked about unescorted. The conservative press attacked them as **nihilists** (those who believe in nothing). In the streets, people whistled and howled at them, jeering: 'Hey you with short hair, disembowelled many corpses recently?'

But women who had escaped from 'family **despotism**' were used to hearing insults. Alexandra Kornilova, one young woman student, said that she and her friends wanted to liberate themselves from the stagnant past and all tradition, from the family and from the marital authority that had enslaved them and prevented them from entering the broad path of self-development and work for the good of society.

6 By the end of the 1860s several high schools and evening courses had been opened for women. But for a woman to aspire at this time to an education and a profession made her a laughing-stock. Besides, the standard of teaching was low, grants almost non-existent, and women students, many still young and inexperienced and from poor families, had to suffer continual harassment in order to attend.

Get up at 8…drink coffee, arrive at school at 9. As soon as the first lecture's over, we race to the porter's lodge, throw on our coats and rush to the other building to get a seat in the front row. Lectures are over by 3 or 4. We all go to the eating house, then go home, work till 5…We have tea at 7, take a short rest, then start work again. Bed is no earlier than 12. *Woman student's diary*

Of 89 women students in St Petersburg in 1872, 12 died before graduation, 8 of tuberculosis and 1 of smallpox. Two killed themselves. One died during the final examination itself.

7 Many grew convinced that the only way to change their society was through revolution, so they abandoned their studies for political work. They were **populists**, that is, they believed that the 'people' (the peasants) were already socialist because of the communal way they divided up their land and reached decisions; they needed only guidance and encouragement

Kursistka (The Girl Student) by Nikolai A. Oschenko, 1883. This painting hangs in the Kiev Museum of Art

to make a revolution. Throughout the 1870s men and women started going 'to the people', as doctors, teachers and **propagandists**.

8 In the 1860s, the populists had seen **women's liberation** as central to their vision of a better, more just world. By the 1870s, however, the question of women's rights had been buried under the weight of other issues. Most women put their own needs to one side when they became revolutionaries. They renounced everything to which they might have aspired – comfort and happiness, secure family life, personal and professional ambition. The sacrifice of their personal ideals gave their commitment to the revolution an extraordinary intensity.

And this was why, when mass arrests made peaceful propaganda impossible, a number of women joined the new People's Will Party, formed in 1879 and dedicated to killing the

The execution in 1881 of Sofia Perovskaya and others implicated in the plot to assassinate Alexander II

German philosopher Karl Marx, 1818–83; a drawing by N. Zhukhov

Tsar. A woman, Sofia Perovskaya, was one of the main organisers of the **assassination**.

9 The ideas of the German philosopher, Karl Marx, had great influence throughout Europe at the end of the nineteenth century. Marx wrote that every development in history was the result of the struggle between classes – the haves and the have-nots: those who own the wealth and those who produce it, the exploiters and the exploited. This inequality was the source of all others, he said, including that between men and women.

Marx described the *capitalist* system as both cruelly unjust and terribly wasteful. Society's wealth was held in the hands of the employers (the capitalist class), who lived off the people who produced it (the working class, or *proletariat*). The interests of workers and employers were completely opposed, and the sooner the workers took over the factories and shared out the wealth between them the better it would be for society as a whole.

1

'To the people!'

With Alexander's reforms and the emancipation of the serfs, new energies burst forth. **Radical** journals appeared. Students, aristocrats and artisans all met together and discussed long and passionately the possibilities for a new and better society. Changes were desperately needed, and every institution, including the old family, was scrutinised and found wanting. To produce a better society, people were now saying, family relations would have to be made more equal and honest, and women would have a fundamental part to play in building the new society. Discussions raged about family life and the role of women – what came to be known as the 'woman question'.

Some women wanted to liberalise family life, and give women more opportunities in the world outside. More radical women wanted to free themselves altogether:

I hadn't the slightest desire to marry anyone. I despised ladies' men and pitied the students who were mothers, absorbed by childcare and petty household concerns. Courtship seemed either coarse or ridiculous to me. *Alexandra Kornilova*

And some preferred to work for social and political revolution in Russia and postpone discussion of the 'woman question' until afterwards. But, for many women, all three approaches were equally important and ensured that the 'woman question' was the burning issue of the day. There could be no improvements in Russia, they believed, without women's liberation. That first phase of the revolution was a time of wonderful optimism.

But the government was stronger than they were – and the old attitudes to women were more persistent than the revolutionaries had imagined. In the 1870s, hundreds of revolutionaries were rounded up and thrown into jail. Increasing numbers were forced to go underground to hide from the police. The 'woman question' now took second place to the struggle against the Tsar, his government and the entire social order in Russia.

Sofia Perovskaya, a leading organiser of Alexander II's assassination

Vera Figner, an active revolutionary, 1880

Workers from a blast-furnace living in overcrowded barrack accommodation, 1905

Women revolutionaries

Hundreds of women took part in the revolutionary struggle of the 1870s, and were particularly selfless and brave. And, having already given up family life and domestic security, they were prepared to sacrifice their own happiness, and even their lives, to the cause of the revolution.

For these women the greatest danger was being trapped in family life and housework. A novelist called Nadezhda Khvoshchina rejected family happiness as

the vulgar happiness of locked-up house, neat and tidy. They seem to smile a welcome at the outsider, but give him nothing but that smug, stupid smile.

Indeed they played down their own feelings to the point where they denied that women had different needs from men. Only a revolution could bring about the sort of society in which women could live freely and happily as the equals of men. To struggle in the meantime for their own equality seemed to them both selfish and irrelevant.

Several women, Sofia Perovskaya, Vera Figner, Anna Yakimova and Tatiana Lebedeva, for instance, played an active part in the assassination of Alexander II in 1881. But they were exceptions. Most women allowed themselves to take the least interesting jobs – while the men got on with the organising and writing.

Revolutionaries and factory workers

The revolutionaries of the 1860s believed that it was the peasants who would make the revolution. By the 1890s these peasants, driven by poverty, had flocked into the towns to work in the new factories. The revolutionaries recognised that workers in the factories were more receptive to revolutionary ideas than the peasants working in the fields.

Many worked fourteen, sixteen, sometimes eighteen hours a day. Often, after work, they simply dropped exhausted on the ground beside their machines. Some lived in filthy, overcrowded barracks provided by their employers. Workers with families lived piled on top of one another in one room, and just a board or curtain up to divide them. Some managed to find lodgings in the outskirts of the town, paying high rents for poor quarters.

In these conditions people who had been peasants tried to make some sort of life for themselves. Several generations of people would live together – fathers, mothers, cousins, children – and many women left the villages and joined their menfolk simply to cook, wash and sew for them. But many women also came to work in the factories.

Workers from the Gubner factory in the late nineteenth century

Women factory workers

Russian women had always been accustomed to extremely hard labour – in the fields, in the mines and in the home – but the factory woman's life was quite unbearably hard. Her wages were about half those of the men. She was often under-nourished. She was frequently the victim of sexual harassment from her employers, rudeness from the men she worked with, and violence and beatings from her menfolk at home. She worked all through her pregnancies too, sometimes right up to the time she went into labour. As a mother, though, she was liable to lose her job, so once the baby was born there was a temptation to kill or abandon it. The alternative was to leave it at home with older children or hand it over to a baby-minder (known as a 'baby-farmer'). Thousands of babies died of malnutrition. Babies sent back to the villages, however, stood a better chance of surviving, so many women would take them back, visiting them when they returned in the summer to bring in the harvest.

Women were slower than the men to leave the countryside to work in the towns; they kept their connection with the villages longer; and at work they were slower to protest. But once their anger was aroused they protested with extraordinary courage – and often with violence – against the conditions of their working lives.

Women in the strike movement

Between 1870 and 1879 there were 176 strikes, most of them in the textile mills, where anything from a quarter to half the workers were women. In tobacco factories, where a large proportion of the workers were women, the foul conditions caused many women to suffer from heart ailments, asthma, migraines, cramps and distended pupils. In 1878 women from two St Petersburg tobacco factories could take no more and marched out. The employers greeted them with threats and obscenities, and the women marched straight back and threw everything out of the windows.

After many such confrontations over the next few years, the first Factory Act was passed in 1882, forbidding the employment of children under twelve. Most employers ignored it, and strikes continued in this spontaneous and explosive manner into the 1890s.

In 1895, 1,500 women at St Petersburg's Laferme cigarette factory, driven to the end of their tether by the introduction of **piece-rates** and the employers' mistreatment of them, rushed through the factory smashing equipment and breaking windows. Then they ran outside where they shouted out their grievances to passers-by. After this demonstration, their demands were partly met – although the employers had at first threatened to throw them all out on the streets.

11

In May 1896 a wave of strikes swept through the textile mills along St Petersburg's Obvodnoi Canal and Neva River – the first 'mass strike' in Russian history. In these mills something like four workers in every ten were women, and as strike followed strike it soon became clear that the women were as angry and militant as the men.

This strike movement had a big influence on revolutionaries – particularly the women. Until then women revolutionaries like Elena Stasova, Nadezhda Krupskaya and Alexandra Kollontai had felt very unsure of themselves. Now they derived new courage and new hope from the striking workers.

It was wonderful to see the politically naive factory girl, hopelessly bowed down by unbearably harsh working conditions, despised by all, now fighting for the rights of the working class and the liberation of women. *Alexandra Kollontai*

Revolutionaries now did all they could to support the strikers: collecting funds, distributing leaflets – and organising meetings even though these were illegal. They hoped that these strikes would eventually bring down the government.

While women continued to come out on strike, very few of them attended meetings or classes. This was in part due to their lack of confidence. Most women workers were illiterate. They were wary of standing up in a public place and exposing their ignorance in front of others – especially men, many of whom resented women working in the factories and had little time for women's problems.

More important, though, were the additional pressures women had to cope with outside work. They were still expected to carry out the traditional household duties – cleaning, cooking, washing and childcare. For many women, this double burden made talk of improving working conditions pointless. Like most socialists, they held the view that the time to think about personal and social issues was *after* the revolution.

Revolutionaries were now getting together to read the works of Karl Marx (see Introduction), the German philosopher. In 1895 the first **marxist** organisation in Russia, the Union of Struggle for the Liberation of the Working Class, was formed – one of whose leaders was Vladimir Ilich Lenin. Marx argued that the capitalist system degraded all human relationships and brought special hardships to women. But despite everything, he said, women's entry into the workforce was a positive step, for only when women and men came out on strike together would the strike movement be strong.

The strike movement crushed

By June 1896 the strike storm had passed. A quarter of a million workers and countless intellectuals had opposed the authorities; thousands of revolutionaries and workers were rounded up, imprisoned, or banished to Siberia. The government dealt harshly with the strikers, and many of them suffered unemployment and police harassment for the rest of their lives. Revolutionaries went underground, forging false identity papers, and assuming disguises in order to hide from the police.

Nadezhda Krupskaya: the impact of factory women on strike in the 1890s gave her and her fellow revolutionaries renewed strength

The Union of Struggle for the Liberation of the Working Class, 1895 – the first marxist organisation in Russia. (Lenin is seated, centre)

Women revolutionaries were less liable to be arrested, however; the authorities failed to take them seriously – especially if they dressed elegantly, as 'ladies'. So during these terrible times more and more women were drawn into setting up workers' literacy schemes, night classes, Sunday Schools and poverty-relief organisations. Through these ventures they were able to combine charity work and fund-raising with a more political kind of education. At night classes they soon became skilful at presenting the ideas of marxism and revolution under the harmless guise of arithmetic or geography lessons, despite the presence of police spies. At meetings called by the poverty-relief organisations they were able to distribute political pamphlets with titles such as *Who Lives on What?* and *The Workers' Day*.

Revolutionaries defend women workers

During 1900 and 1901 the number of women working in factories increased by 12,000 and the number of men decreased by 13,000. Large numbers of male workers had been sacked for striking, and women, still regarded by employers as less likely to strike, were regularly used to replace them.

Factory owners everywhere are replacing men with women, not only amongst adults but also amongst the young, believing the female element to be more docile and steady.
Contemporary factory report

The large number of new women workers in the factories increased the men's anger against them.

13

First issue of the illegal marxist newspaper Iskra, December 1900

The revolutionaries were the only people to pay serious attention to women's working conditions. They did so in the first issue of their new paper *Iskra* (Spark), which came out in 1900, and which spoke to the men and women working in Russia's factories. It was published in Geneva, Switzerland, where Lenin and various other revolutionaries were then living in exile. (It would have been illegal to publish such a paper in Russia.)

A vast network of people was involved in smuggling this paper out of Switzerland into Russia and into the factories (where it had to be read in secret, since anyone seen with a copy would have been arrested). A number of women were part of the *Iskra* chain of command; they were especially valued for their attention to detail, their reliability and dedication, and their attendance to correspondence. Elena Stasova was particularly highly regarded as an *Iskrovka*, or *Iskra* agent – and was known to her associates as 'Comrade Absolute'. She and Nadezhda Krupskaya were experts at memorising names and messages, inventing codes and cracking them, concocting invisible ink and arranging secret meeting-places.

With the appearance of *Iskra*, revolutionaries eventually started to make some contact with women workers. Women themselves now started writing to the paper from the factories and mills about their dreary and exhausting lives. In issue after issue the paper explained to men and women workers that they both had the same interest in fighting the Tsar and the bosses, and it gave special attention to cases of women workers taking part in strikes.

It was still very hard for revolutionaries to speak to any but the most militant factory women. After an eighteen-hour day at her work-bench, the newly recruited woman worker would generally return to her barracks with no desire but for sleep, and no explanation offered for her life other than that she had somehow deserved God's wrath.

14

2

A new upsurge of anger

More women drawn into the struggle

In the spring of 1901, when workers poured onto the streets of St Petersburg in a series of angry riots and strikes, women joined the street-fighting for the first time. Women, too, met head-on with the police, and were left wounded or dead. During the workers' defence of the Nevsky district an eighteen-year-old girl ran out of one of the factories and began handing cobblestones to the men. 'We stand by our men!' she was heard to shout. In the larger demonstrations throughout Southern Russia later that year, hundreds of women fought in the streets alongside the men; and along with the men were shot down, flogged and thrown into jail.

People's anger was aroused now – yet their living conditions were unchanged. What was to be done? Many revolutionaries decided that the only answer was to kill prominent members of the government. In 1901 the Socialist Revolutionary Party was formed. Its members believed, like those of its predecessors in the People's Will Party, that it was the peasants who would bring about a revolution. One section of the party was committed to persuading the peasants to a programme of agrarian reforms. The other section of the party was the Fighting Organisation, and this was committed to revenge killings. Large numbers of women became Socialist Revolutionaries.

The Marxists, however, were deeply opposed to terrorism; they believed that workers must simply organise their resistance more effectively, in order to avoid police bullets, prison and exile. They realised that revolutionaries would have to adopt more secret ways of working, and would have to form a smaller, more disciplined, illegal party.

It was in 1902, as more and more workers and revolutionaries were going into hiding to avoid the police, that Lenin produced his famous pamphlet *What Is To Be Done?* In this and in articles for *Iskra*, he described his vision of the party that would lead the revolution. It would be one of intellectuals, full-time revolutionaries, who would support the workers in their war against the employers, and encourage this to develop into a mass strike of the whole population. At this point the workers could take over the factories, force the capitalists and the Tsar to step down, and form a new government, which would run society fairly, without making a profit out of anyone's labour.

At the Second **Russian Social Democratic Labour Party** (RSDLP) Congress in Brussels, Lenin's group within the party, the **Bolsheviks** (= the majority), who wanted a small, disciplined party, outvoted the **Menshevik** group (= the minority), who wanted a larger party comprising anyone who would support its aims. For many Social Democrats, however, the differences between the two did not seem that great.

But even as revolutionaries were debating, Southern Russia was in the grip of peasant uprisings and workers' strikes, and as riots and strikes continued into the following year, more and more men and women were drawn to the social democrats. Many were attracted by the Mensheviks' idea of a larger more spontaneous party and many women felt that the Mensheviks were more sympathetic to their cause. Others joined the Bolsheviks, feeling that only they had the dedication and determination capable of developing the sort of party that could lead the workers to revolution. The strike movement was gathering force again; and now it was intensifying to the point where workers appeared to be threatening the basis of Nicholas II's state. Increasing numbers of women were participating too.

Indeed about a third of all workers being employed now were women. Despite this **most women were still avoiding life and struggle...believing their destiny to be the cooking pot, the washtub and the cradle.** *Alexandra Kollontai*

And from one militant factory woman:

'**The masses of the workers held that politics wasn't a woman's business. Her business was at** home, with the children, the nappies and the pots and pans...' *Quoted by Vera Karelina.*

The Russo-Japanese War

What finally changed things was the outbreak of war with Japan, early in 1904. Sixteen months later most of the Russian fleet had been sunk. The Russian defeat was crushing, the peace terms humiliating; people's lives became desperately hard. Throughout 1904, as men were sent off to war, peasant women found they could not support themselves and their children by working alone on their plots of land. Desperate for work, thousands of them set off for the towns – where most of them, as usual, ended up in filthy sweat-shops or factories, which usually did not even pay a living wage. Many could not get even this kind of degrading, low-paid work, and were forced to become prostitutes. (Politically active women were becoming increasingly concerned to alleviate the dreadful hardships that drove such women into prostitution.) But many peasant women who left home for the first time left their ignorance behind them for ever:

They hurried to the towns to tread the corridors of government institutions in the hope of news of a husband, a son or a father, to stick up for their allowances and to fight for various other rights... They returned to the villages in a sober, hardened mood. *Alexandra Kollontai*

Angry and hungry, peasant women banded together to attack the landlords. This was the start of the famous 'peasant women's riots' (**babi bunty**, in Russian), which continued all through 1904. Women set fire to barns, raided manor houses, smashed farm tools. **Cossacks** were sent galloping into the villages to put down the riots. They continued, despite savage reprisals by the Cossacks.

In the cities the terrorists continued to pursue and kill unpopular members of the government. The workers too were in a hard and angry mood. In that year alone 1 in every 49 metal-workers was killed in an accident – as were 500 railway-workers. The misery of the people was no longer bearable.

Group of Cossack soldiers

Bloody Sunday

The spark that finally set tsarist Russia on fire was the strike on 3 January 1905 at St Petersburg's huge Putilov armaments factory. Two days later the strike had spread to the shipyards. Then the bakers came out in support. That week the workers of St Petersburg decided to march to the Winter Palace, to hand the Tsar a petition.

On 9 January, 200,000 men and women, dressed in their Sunday best and accompanied by children and elderly relatives, moved off in respectful silence to the Winter Palace, bearing portraits of the Tsar.

Sire! *read their petition,* **We working men of St Petersburg, our wives, our children and our parents, aged and helpless men and women, have come to you, our ruler, in search of justice and protection...**

They stood outside the Tsar's palace for two hours in the snow, joking and stamping their feet to keep warm. Then from the clear blue sky a shot rang out. Then another. Suddenly

Cossacks were galloping into the palace square, shooting wildly at the crowd. That day about 300 people were killed.

That day also killed people's faith in a just Tsar, and was the start of a great mass movement against the old tsarist regime.

Strikes and riots

Following the events of Bloody Sunday, strikes, demonstrations and riots broke out all over Russia. In these heady days all the hardships and struggles that men and women had gone through brought them closer together. Until then women revolutionaries had tended to do comparatively lowly (though crucial) jobs: putting messages into code and ensuring their delivery, organising secret hideouts and meeting-places, and all the other extremely sensitive tasks to do with underground communication.

Now, however, women who joined the revolutionary movement were taking the initiative themselves. In St Petersburg the Tsar summoned a delegation of workers to tell them to elect representatives to a commission to investigate their grievances. They did so, and a number of women were elected. When the Tsar refused to find seats for the women they organised an angry protest demonstration in the name of all the city's working women – and the men supported them.

Working men *could* be made to abandon old prejudices if women took the initiative, yet women still had to fight a great deal of grumbling from the men when they insisted on joining strike committees. Even though almost a third of the workers in Russia were women, the additional demands on their time removed them from the social life of the strike movement. Their illiteracy cut them off from the political pamphlets and strike leaflets that were circulated in the factories.

'Bloody Sunday' outside the Winter Palace, 1905.

17

For the people who wrote these leaflets, women might as well have been invisible.

There wasn't a single mention of the woman worker…It was just as though she were non-existent, like some sort of appendage.
Vera Karelina

And because women felt so invisible, they were still frightened of speaking up at meetings.

Well yes, I do want to express myself, *admitted one woman worker to Vera Karelina,* **but then I think it over – so many people will be watching me, and what if someone laughs at me? I grow cold with terror at the thought.**

As strikes, demonstrations and riots continued, the government retaliated and Russia turned into a bloodbath. Whole villages were killed, Jews and people from other ethnic minorities were massacred, hundreds of people were thrown into jail. Yet month after month, in town after town, workers continued to come out on strike for shorter working hours and better conditions. And more and more women were now shaking off their old docility, leaving their machines, and giving the strike movement a completely new sense of solidarity and confidence.

Women make their own demands

Women were beginning to insist that their own needs be recognised in the strike demands, and they had the support of some working men. Strike leaflets were beginning to reflect these demands: paid maternity leave (four weeks before the birth and six weeks after), time off during the day to feed infants, and the provision of nurseries at factories. A few strikers went so far as to demand time off for women to do the laundry and housework; a few even wanted equal pay for women. But there were still all too many strike leaflets which appealed to workers to 'behold your endless toil and your wife's tears'.

It was in 1901 that Nadezhda Krupskaya, a Social Democrat (and Lenin's wife), had written and helped to smuggle a booklet called *The Woman Worker* into the factories. But since then little else had been produced for women factory workers. Throughout 1905 men and women in the revolutionary movement were working flat out to support the strikers in every

way they could. But it was all too sadly obvious how little they concerned themselves with the lives of working women, and how inadequate was their interest in women's liberation.

Most Social Democrats (most of them men) regarded women as the 'backward section' of the population, and believed it was up to men to educate and liberate them. And of course, once private property and capitalism had been abolished, they believed, women would automatically be the equals of men anyway. A few Bolsheviks and Mensheviks, however, were now beginning to insist that women should liberate themselves, and not wait for men – or the revolution – to do it for them. They considered that men's unwillingness to treat them as equals in the revolutionary struggle, or to deal seriously with them, was a continuation of the treatment they had always endured. If working women's needs were not listened to, those women would go off and look elsewhere for support. This threatened the revolutionary movement with the loss of large numbers of valuable recruits.

And in fact this was starting to happen. In April 1905 a group of St Petersburg society women joined together to campaign for propertied women's right to jobs, education and the vote. They appealed to women workers to support them – with considerable success. So Alexandra Kollontai and some Bolshevik women weavers went along to the inaugural meeting of this new Union of Women's Equality. Propertied and working women had nothing in common, they said. The class war was spreading. Here were wealthy women campaigning to improve their already privileged status, and factory women would certainly not do themselves any good by supporting them. It was the economic system that created the inequality between rich and poor, men and women. Women could not hope to be the equals of men without a revolution that destroyed the old society and made a better one in its place. To pretend otherwise was a middle-class dream. So working women should join the Bolshevik party instead – where they belonged – and fight for their rights within it.

Their words were evidently not lost, for

Members of the Bolshevik party who took part in the 1905 revolution. Elena Stasova is sitting in the middle row, two to the right of Lenin. However, there is a noticeable lack of women

many women workers did join the Bolsheviks that April. But Kollontai and her friends felt that these working women had been recruited under false pretences for the Bolshevik party, which claimed to have women's interests at heart, 'did not know then how to use them, how to awaken their independence and class consciousness'.

In demanding more discussion of women's matters within the Bolshevik party, Kollontai also had to be careful to avoid being accused of trying to divert working women's attention from the task ahead: to unseat the Tsar, take over the factories and proclaim the socialist revolution.

3

Women in the 1905 revolution

Women revolutionaries

The strikes and riots of 1905 hit more than a hundred towns, drew in more than a million workers, and turned thousands of women into revolutionaries.

Throughout that summer the looting and burning of landlords' estates continued. When Cossack soldiers were sent in to suppress the riots, women joined together to fight back.

Many women joined the Socialist Revolutionary Party (then in its heyday), and carried out, on their own or with men, assassinations of government officials. As new prisons were built to house those jailed for terrorist offences, one prison governor remarked: 'In terms of criminality and the urge to escape, the women are no different from the men.'

In the towns, employers still preferred to employ women, believing them to be more submissive than men, less likely to swear, smoke or come out on strike. But now this image was changing. Eleven thousand women textile-workers came out on strike that summer in Ivanovo-Voznesensk, near Moscow, in one of the largest strikes ever seen in Russia. Twenty-eight of them were killed by the police.

Striking workers at Yartsevo in Smolensk. In 1905 thousands of workers came out on strike

The Soviet and the Manifesto

Strikes became more frequent and intense. On 8 October there was a rail strike in Moscow, with strikers putting up barricades to defend themselves against the soldiers' bullets. The St Petersburg rail junction was hit next. Factory workers were in a fighting mood. It was then that the most important workers' council, or *Soviet*, was born. The Soviet's immediate purpose, when delegates first met in St Petersburg on 14 October, was to direct a general strike. Its more long-term purpose was to develop into a genuine workers' government, which would ultimately replace that of the Tsar. The government began to fear for its existence.

On that day, 14 October, St Petersburg's governor, General Trepov, sent troops into the capital and ordered them to fire on striking workers with the words: 'No blank volleys and do not spare the cartridges!'

Three days later, Trepov's troops broke up a session of the Soviet. The delegates declared that the strike would continue. And on that day, for the first time in Russian history, the Tsar responded to people's rage not with bullets but with the offer of reforms: a parliament (or **Duma**), and a **manifesto** which promised more liberty.

It was not long, however, before people were being thrown into prison for making use of this new liberty, and the Tsar's parliament failed to satisfy even the conservatives. But the 'days of freedom' that followed did at least provide a brief breathing space. Trade unions sprang up, workers' clubs opened and Bolsheviks and Mensheviks agreed to bury their differences* in a newly reunited Social Democratic Party.

The Union of Women's Equality and their campaign for the vote

Members of the Union of Women's Equality had high hopes in the Duma, and expected that propertied women would soon be given the vote and allowed to stand in this new parliament. They therefore started to make contact with women in the factories, urging them to support their campaign to enter the Duma. Once there, they promised, they would fight for freer divorce laws, and an end to state-licensed prostitution, militarism and the death penalty.

This inspiring programme – and the promise of a movement to unite women of all classes – had a tremendous appeal for many working women, and hundreds of them signed the Union's petition for the vote. But when it was presented to the Duma it was jeered at, pushed aside and forgotten. The Union, undaunted, continued their campaign for the vote.

The Bolsheviks had boycotted the Duma as a waste of time. Tsarism could not be 'liberalised', they said; it must be abolished. They considered that it was dishonest of the Union of Women's Equality to propose reforms without recognising that in Russia a revolution would be needed to bring them about. The Union was simply out to set working men and women against one another, they said, and to create difficulties and divisions within the working class. What they would not admit, though, was that these difficulties and divisions had existed as long as men and women had worked in the factories together, and merely calling for a united party was no way to resolve them.

---

* The alliance lasted until 1912, although the old differences remained – with the Bolsheviks continuing to insist on a smaller, more disciplined party, and the Mensheviks calling for the broadest possible coalition with all those opposed to the present order in Russia.

Women and family life

Family life, and men's and women's attitudes to each other, were changed dramatically by the 1905 revolution and its aftermath. People did not live twenty-four hours on the barricades, after all; their lives at home did not merely fade into the background, as many revolutionaries seemed to wish. On the contrary, the 1905 revolution was for many people a confusing and intensely felt mixture of happiness and tragedy, fear and exhilaration. 1905 changed people's lives in ways that were both painful and marvellous.

Hundreds of women, suspicious of the Union of Women's Equality organised their own trade unions instead, and joined the Bolsheviks or Mensheviks. But once in the revolutionary movement they found they were expected to put aside all the problems they experienced as women – for such things were not regarded as 'political'. No sooner had they returned from a long day at the factory than they were expected by their comrades in the revolutionary movement to drop everything – leaving the children unwashed, the dinner uncooked – and go out to a meeting. While from their husbands there might be beatings and insults if the house was not clean and the dinner was not on the table.

But a few women were now joining the Social Democrats and insisting that men take account of their needs. There was too much talk of armed revolution, they said, not enough of the needs and feelings of the men and women *making* that revolution. In practical terms, this meant first of all that housework must be shared. Who did the washing-up and who cared for the children were in fact *political* issues, just as important as who took over the government and who ran the factories. Men could not be expected automatically to change their attitudes to women *after* the revolution. It was clear that men and women together would have to make a start *now* at working out better, more equal relationships. They believed that the new society they were fighting to create depended upon it.

Some women did try to raise these issues at meetings, but were silenced by the men. There were centuries of maltreatment and oppression to be overcome.

21

Fighting on the barricades in 1905, from a painting by Vladimirov

Bolshevik attitudes to women

The 'days of freedom' were short-lived. People soon grew afraid to strike and meetings were regularly infiltrated by police. Numerous revolutionaries were arrested or fled the country. Bolshevik membership dwindled, and more and more Bolsheviks were forced underground. For a great many of them, this furtive life and the constant fear of arrest had a very damaging effect.

They remembered how the strikes of 1896 had been crushed. They remembered the haphazard way in which the revolution of 1905 had arisen – and the ease with which that too was crushed. And they insisted that next time there must be an organised party to lead the revolution. The hardships of revolutionaries working underground forced them to adopt a particularly inflexible political style, and an intimidating stress on the need for discipline and intellectual brilliance, which operated particularly against women – especially those with husbands and children.

Women's clubs

Mocked and thwarted by their comrades, some Bolshevik women got together and organised their own meetings, at which women could discuss some of the things that particularly concerned them.

A number of workers' clubs had opened in 1905, and were allowed to operate legally. It was in these clubs that Alexandra Kollontai and a group of women textile-workers decided to hold a series of meetings. Male club-members objected to the rooms being used for these meetings and tore down posters advertising the events in order deliberately to mislead the women wishing to attend. Despite all the difficulties, however, a few women's meetings were held, under the guise of literacy classes, so as not to attract the attentions of the police. (There was often a policewoman in the audience, so women had to be told about the risks involved in attending.)

About twenty-five or thirty women would meet at any one time. As there was almost no suitable literature available (apart from Krupskaya's pamphlet, *The Woman Worker*, written four years earlier), the teachers had rapidly to develop and illustrate the themes of exploitation and revolution in such a way as to capture their audience's sympathy.

These meetings were in fact very similar to the workers' night classes organised by the Union of Struggle in the 1890s. Then, however, there had been no women in the audience. Then, the classes had been regarded as a vital way of developing workers' political knowledge and negotiating skills. Now, the party was too engrossed in its 'urgent political tasks' to help the women find premises, literature and speakers. Most organisers had little experience of the sort of caution needed for this kind of propaganda, and many were arrested. There was also continuing disruption from male club-members.

Eventually, the Bolsheviks agreed to allow women to meet in order to discuss setting up some sort of women's organisation within the party itself. But when the women arrived at the hall where the meeting was to be held they found a note pinned to the door saying: 'Meeting for women only postponed. Meeting for men only tomorrow'. Incidents like this made many women lose heart. They decided they were not strong enough to organise on their own, and started attending men's clubs instead. Others started attending meetings organised by the Union of Women's Equality, who were still pressing ahead with their campaign for the vote. But a group of working women from St Petersburg's textile union, alarmed by the Union's success, managed to persuade the Bolsheviks to support another series of women's meetings.

These meetings opened in the spring of 1907 in the sumptuous mansion of the philanthropic Nobel family. They were immediately immensely popular.

The atmosphere was electric…The large hall was filled to overflowing with women from the textile and needlewomen's unions, textile-workers and factory-workers…
Alexandra Kollontai

The women would listen to twenty-minute talks on maternity care, or factory hygiene – the teachers using just a few minutes at the end to make their political message. The policewomen in the audience were surprisingly unsuspicious. However, they were sometimes zealous and made their presence felt. At such times, the speaker would rely on a single word or gesture to make her point.

One meeting coincided with a strike at a nearby factory, and the audience poured onto the street to put the teacher's words into practice. The police drove them away, and although there were no arrests, the meetings were banned from then on.

The Women's Mutual Aid Club

By now, pressure from women in the party had forced the Bolsheviks to support women-only meetings, and by the winter of 1907 women had their own club, the Women's Mutual Aid Club, which opened at the headquarters of the St Petersburg textile union.

It was open every evening. One room was set aside for a cheap buffet, so women working nearby could drop in for sandwiches and stay for lectures. Another room was a library. A summer camp was organised, to enable women who all too rarely had a holiday to get away in the summer. Membership was open to men, but it was women who were responsible for running it; and on opening night the club was packed with women. Soon about two hundred women and men were regularly arriving to use the library, meet friends in the buffet and attend lectures on socialist campaigns and women's movements in Russia and abroad.

But it was not long before the club began to run into problems. Many Bolshevik men had disliked the venture from the start. At a time when the workers' movement needed to be strong, they said, women's clubs merely weakened the movement by producing bad feelings between men and women. They demanded that the club should be closed down, and started packing the meetings to heckle and argue their case. Women soon grew weary of having to defend their club against these arguments. Party members were determined to stop them doing anything on their own.

The First All-Russian Women's Congress

A group of St Petersburg society women were in no such danger, however, when in the winter of 1908 they started organising a women's congress. It was to be a formal, ticket-only affair, attended by about a thousand women. The audience would be drawn from such respectable, long-established women's charitable organisations as the Russian Society for the Protection of Russian Women, the Society for the Protection of Young Girls and the Women's Mutual Philanthropic Society, involved mainly in the campaign against prostitution. Also attending would be members of the Union of Women's Equality and its offshoot the Women's Progressive Party, which also campaigned for the vote but, unlike the Union, refused to work with men. They were to hear reports on the campaign for votes for women and on attempts to improve women's working conditions; but the number of working women actually invited was very small, and there was much angry talk of it amongst the organisers' own servants and laundresses (who were not invited).

As the day of the congress drew closer, a group of about forty-five factory women and domestic servants, increasingly eager to 'scandalise the feminists', began to meet every day after work, often under the innocent guise of birthday parties or sewing bees, and over the cakes or embroidery they would practise the speeches they were to make at the congress.

The day before the congress opened, the organisers went to visit these women in their homes, bearing sweets and fruit and advising them not to attend. And the following day they were equally daunting, seated on a stage bright with flowers and adorned with a large banner that proclaimed: 'One Women's Movement for All Women!'

The women in the 'labour group', red carnations pinned to their dresses, were shaking with nerves in the anxiety to get their lines right. But as each item on the agenda was discussed – women at work, women in the political parties, women and the vote – they stepped up to the stage with increasing boldness, and one by one they delivered their statements. Their speech on sickness benefit caused an uproar, with women on the platform hissing and stamping, and women in the labour group jumping up to shout: 'What do you know of our lives? Bowling along in your carriages while we get splashed by the mud!'

The congress collapsed in chaos. The following day the hall was swarming with police; thirteen members of the labour group were arrested, and the organisers were subjected to a humiliating body search. One politician likened the event to 'an assembly of whores'. Similar insults followed, and for the next six years or so the middle-class women's movement could no longer count on support in high places.

The reaction to the revolution

The savage reaction against the women's movement was a part of the general reaction to the defeated revolution. The following year the Empress Alexandra, whose views had a great influence on the Tsar, sponsored a conference for 'purely Russian women' to offset the feminists' congress of 1908; she knew very well that the traditional values of Russian life had to be kept if Russia was to avoid a revolution and the monarchy was to survive.

People suffered in various terrible ways from the reaction that now set in in earnest. Any serious discussion of women's liberation tended to be drowned in a craze for brutality. Numerous pornographic books appeared, there was an epidemic of murders, prostitutes were attacked and various sordid sex clubs opened – and all this often in the name of 'sexual freedom', 'free love' and 'sexual equality'. For many Bolsheviks, reluctant at the best of times to discuss women's needs, any discussion of sexual attitudes now seemed doubly suspicious.

Even those living in the comparative safety of exile had their problems. About half the Bolshevik exiles in Paris, where Lenin and his wife Nadezhda Krupskaya were based, were women. Krupskaya was an editor of the Bolsheviks' newspaper; another woman, Inessa Armand, was responsible for keeping all the Bolshevik exiles in Europe in touch with each other; and many other women were doing equally difficult and dangerous jobs. Yet when they tried to organise meetings for working women in Paris, they met with such opposition from their male comrades that they gave up the idea. Women were still expected to keep in the background, to let men take the initiative and stifle their own desires. They had to be very brave indeed to stand up for themselves; but there were many of them who did.

4

Sisters and comrades

International Women's Day

At a congress of the Second **International** in Copenhagen in 1910, women decided to make one day a year an occasion for women throughout the world to celebrate and demonstrate. The day chosen was 8 March, and on International Women's Day the following year thousands of women demonstrated in the towns and villages of Germany. Many were arrested and demonstrations were broken up violently by the police. But despite this, 8 March soon became an important date in every socialist's calendar, a day for women to celebrate their strength and militancy.

Indeed in Germany, while the Kaiser built ever more warships and the socialist party entered into an electoral alliance with the liberals, it was the women in that party who were particularly courageous in warning people of the impending war and urging men to resist being conscripted. On 8 March 1913, women held huge anti-war demonstrations throughout Germany.

In that year women in Russia celebrated International Women's Day for the first time. In St Petersburg thousands of women took over the Stock Exchange to protest against their hard lives; the police arrived, broke up the demonstration and made numerous arrests. In Moscow, too, women took to the streets, and there were similar angry demonstrations in Kiev, Tiflis and Samara.

Russian women bring out their own newspapers

These demonstrations were well covered by the socialist press. The Bolsheviks' paper *Pravda* (Truth) brought out a special Women's Day issue, with pictures of women strikers and greetings from women abroad, and this inspired so many letters from women all over Russia that it rapidly became clear that women needed a paper of their own. Soon a group of Bolshevik women in exile were corresponding with friends at home with a view to bringing one out and, despite all the difficulties of communication, the first issue of *Rabotnitsa* (Woman Worker) appeared in St Petersburg on International Women's Day 1914. It sold out immediately. All the St Petersburg editors were promptly arrested and the offices were closed. But new offices were found, and new editors, who scraped up enough money from sewing jobs to bring out seven issues. The Mensheviks too brought out a paper for women, *Golos Rabotnitsy* (Woman Worker's Voice). It too was popular amongst women (although only two issues appeared). The appearance of both these papers showed how far both Bolsheviks and Mensheviks had come in their willingness to let women be heard.

Rabotnitsa's new offices were flooded with letters from women complaining about their working conditions, and there were poems too, and stories. After three months *Rabotnitsa* was closed down by the police, but by then thousands of enthusiastic women readers had been drawn to support the Bolsheviks.

Women and war

In July 1914, Russia mobilised troops in defence of Serbia, bringing her allies France and Britain into the First World War against Austria and Germany. During the course of that war, from 1914 to 1918, more than 17 million people from twenty-six countries lost their lives – at least two million (by far the largest number from a single country) were Russian.

By the time Britain declared war on Germany on 4 August 1914, most Russians were gripped by pro-war, anti-German feeling. The only people to stand out against the war were the Bolsheviks.

Within a year over a million Russian soldiers had been killed. Regiments were surrendering en masse. Nicholas II was universally loathed. Living costs soared. Speculation was rampant. And in the cities women were rioting for bread.

As in many European countries, for many women the war had at first held out the promise of greater freedom and more jobs. As men were conscripted and sent to fight, women took over their jobs. Many worked as telegraphists, trolley-drivers and conductors, traffic controllers, janitors and nurses. Many took jobs in the mines and forests. Some even joined the army as soldiers, drivers and – occasionally – pilots. Yet women were still paid less than men for the same jobs, and their conditions at work did not improve. While prices shot up and provisions became more and more scarce, women with husbands at the front (the *soldatki*, or soldiers' wives) found they could not support themselves and their children on their meagre pensions.

Desperate and hungry, women in the cities started to loot the food shops. In April 1915, when the sale of meat was suspended for a day in **St Petersburg** (now renamed Petrograd), women smashed and looted a large meat market. Two days later the same thing happened at bread shops in Moscow, and the governor of the city was badly hurt by cobblestones hurled by angry women. The queues got longer, foodstuffs became even more expensive, and that summer there were more angry riots at Moscow's open-air Khitrovo food market. In June 1915 a strike of women textile-workers at Ivanovo-Voznesensk began as a 'flour strike' to last until flour would be available, and a month later the same women came out on strike demanding an end to the war and the release of jailed workers. Thirty were killed. Another women's strike in Kostroma was crushed violently by the police, and was followed by a massive funeral demonstration and further strike in which women sent a circular to the soldiers asking for their protection.

For most middle-class Russian women, however, pro-war feelings still ran high; they could not bear the idea of a German victory, or the thought that their menfolk were dying for nothing. On International Women's Day in 1916 a group of Bolshevik women students in Petrograd put up a poster that read: 'Working Women! Comrades! This is the day of our solidarity! The government has sent our sons to their death. Now it is time for us to shout:

"Enough blood! Down with war! Bring this criminal government to justice!"' Pro-war women students tore down the poster; it was put up again, and torn down again.

One year later, however, women came out into the streets of the capital to demand an end to the hunger and suffering of the past three years.

The March 1917 revolution begins

In 1917 International Women's Day was celebrated early in Petrograd. When a group of women textile-workers asked the Bolshevik central committee what they should do on that day, they were told not to strike and to 'await party instructions'. But there were no instructions, for the party's press was out of operation. And so women took matters into their own hands, and when workers were locked out of the huge Putilov armaments factory on 7 March, the women of Petrograd took to the streets. By noon women were abandoning the factories and bread-queues and pouring into the centre of the city with rough and ready banners. 'BREAD!' they read; 'OUR CHILDREN ARE STARVING!'

Soon housewives and women workers from the homes and factories on the western side of the city were surging across the Neva bridges and thronging the streets. The *soldatki* joined them, demanding an end to the war. Then women working at the Vasilev Island trolley-bus terminus came out on strike, having first visited the neighbouring barracks of the infantry regiment and won their promise not to shoot. The following day, the numbers of men and women on the streets had swollen to 197,000 and stones and ice were thrown at the police.

Over the next few days women swept through the streets, gathering strength as they went, and encouraging the men to follow them. The soldiers in the Petrograd garrisons, mostly young recruits or family men, refused to go out, and their officers were no keener. Even the Cossacks lost all desire to fight.

Women continued to take the initiative as events moved towards a general strike. By 10 March the women were invading the soldiers' ranks and seizing their guns.

Crowds pouring into the streets of Petrograd in their thousands in food riots, strikes and demonstrations, March 1917

Students fill the streets of Petrograd in March 1917

They go up to the officers more boldly than the men. Taking hold of their rifles they beseech, almost command: 'Put down your guns and join us!' *Leon Trotsky*

Students were leaving lectures now and joining the workers on the streets. There were no trams or newspapers: the strike had become general. The poor working-class district of Vyborg was in the hands of a newly formed Soviet, and the Bolsheviks, the only party to have called for an armed uprising, were now called to put their principles into practice as the workers demanded guns. With almost all the Bolshevik leaders in exile, those remaining in the capital tried helplessly to hold back a revolution that was happening too soon.

The demonstrations became more violent, and several buildings were set on fire. The Red Guards appeared on the streets now. These were teams of men and women armed by the Bolsheviks and supported by women medical assistants called *sanitarki*. On 12 March a group of soldiers rushed the prisons and released a number of jailed revolutionaries. They immediately proclaimed a new government – the Soviet of Workers' and

27

Soldiers' Deputies – then marched off to the Duma to negotiate with its deputies how the two governments might work together.

On 13 March the last remaining troops loyal to the Tsar laid down their guns, and Tsar Nicholas II, recognising that he could no longer control 160,000 mutinous soldiers and a city full of 'criminals', resigned 'in the national interest'.

The Duma formed a new, **Provisional Government** composed of liberal landlords. New ministers (Commissars) were elected to old ministries, and promises were made to run the old ministries, and they promised to restore soldiers' confidence in their officers and to win the war.

In fact, though, this new government which was swept into power was utterly mystified about what it was supposed to do. Prior to March, most of its ministers had been hoping that the Tsar would put himself at the head of a more liberal government, and so avoid the calamity of his abdication. Now they were panic-stricken. Now, they realised, it was ordinary people who held the power and it would not be long before the people toppled this precarious government and put themselves in power.

A postcard showing the ministers of the Provisional Government

5

Women in 1917

The war was dragging on. Living costs were soaring. There were protest demonstrations day and night throughout the cities of Russia. Strikes continued.

The first people to come out on strike after the March revolution were Petrograd's laundresses, toiling away in steamy, filthy underground laundries, plagued by rheumatism and illness. At last they could take no more and stopped work, demanding better pay, shorter hours and the arrest of the laundry-owners. The Provisional Government made various promises to improve matters, then ordered them back. They refused, and held out for their demands.

The leader of the strike was a Bolshevik named Sakharova. And for many other laundresses too, the Bolsheviks' promises of a better life began to seem real, not just the sort of promises all parties made to get themselves elected. The Bolshevik newspaper *Pravda* regularly devoted a page to the progress of the strike, with appeals for financial help and lists of strike-breakers' names. Soon the laundresses were demanding an end to the war too.

From one end of Petrograd to the other men and women were milling about in an endless series of demonstrations and meetings. People were talking and arguing on every street corner; in the Bolsheviks' modest little offices on the Moika Canal (where *Pravda* was published); in the sumptuous palace of the Tsar's mistress, which Bolshevik soldiers had taken over as their headquarters; and in the Tauride Palace, where the Soviet sat day and night.

For now it was the Soviet that held the real power in Petrograd. 'The Provisional Government's orders are not obeyed unless they happen to fall in with the wishes of the Soviet', confessed the government's president, Prince Lvov.

The composition of the Soviet

Who were the people who made up the Soviet? The majority, in the spring of 1917, were

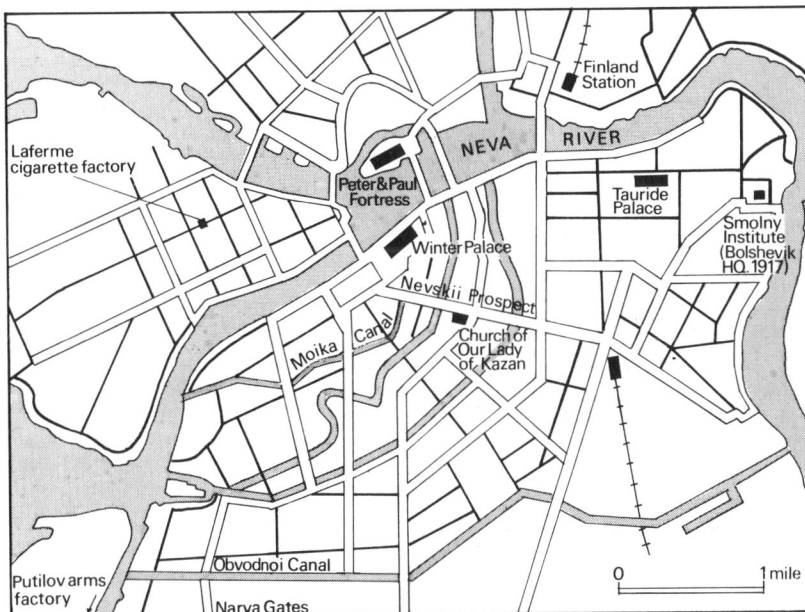

Petrograd in 1917

Mensheviks and Socialist Revolutionaries. To the Mensheviks the March revolution had come as a shock. The workers were not yet ready to seize power, they believed; the Soviet's task was now to make alliances with liberals in the government. To the Socialist Revolutionaries, who enjoyed enormous influence in the countryside, the revolution appeared equally premature; they too believed that the Soviet must strengthen its ties with liberals and businessmen, rather than with the workers. The Bolsheviks were in a minority on the Soviet. Most of their leaders were in exile, and those remaining in Petrograd, like Josef Stalin and Lev Kamenev, had become extremely cautious after long years of working underground. Thus, like the Mensheviks and the Socialist Revolutionaries, they wanted only to act as a kind of loyal opposition to the Provisional Government, and to put pressure on it to make peace with Germany.

Russians were too poor and too uneducated, they believed, to confront the Provisional Government and put in power a more popular one. They should wait instead for the workers of Germany to rise against their Kaiser and demand an end to the war, then Russia would follow her example. For the time being, most Soviet delegates (and the workers and soldiers they represented) felt that this 'dual power' arrangement with the Provisional Government was the best they could hope for.

Until then, there had been almost no women in the Soviet. A regiment of soldiers had eventually decided that they could just as well be represented by a woman as by a man, and had elected Alexandra Kollontai to represent them. Once there, she urged women to elect their own delegates. Men wanted to exclude them, she said, and to keep themselves in power. But women must fight their way in:

We'll never be handed our rights on a plate! We must take them ourselves, and fight for our own interests!

Now Petrograd's *soldatki* started organising their own rations and pensions, and sending their own delegates to the Soviet. Petrograd's housemaids too were meeting in large numbers and electing delegates. 'Comrade maids! We need a bigger hall!' appealed one of them in a *Pravda* article after a meeting had flowed onto

Demonstration of soldatki *in April 1917*

the street. Restaurant workers also formed their own union and elected delegates, after a waitress named 'Comrade Katya' appealed in the *Rabochaya gazeta* (Workers' Paper) for support from 'all women comrades in the tea-rooms of Petrograd'. Women at the Mignon chocolate factory followed suit after protesting to the government about their terrible working conditions, as did workers in the Frolic textile mill, after demanding a 100 per cent wage increase for men, and a 125 per cent increase for women.

Lenin's return to Petrograd

It was not long, however, before hundreds of factories and barracks were sending Bolshevik delegates to the Soviet, and clamouring for peace, bread and land.

On 3 April Lenin and thirty-two other Bolshevik exiles returned to Petrograd. Within a few days many Russians had heard Lenin's rousing message: world war had at last made possible a world revolution, in which the workers of Russia had the honour of striking the first blow, he said. They could now get rid of the Provisional Government and install one that would tear up the old tsarist peace treaties and invite the warring countries to make peace. These bold terms would be impossible for any existing government to accept. But they would seize the imagination of people

30

everywhere, and soldiers of every nation would leave their posts and turn their guns on their governments. And so the war would be turned into an international revolution.

For thousands of men and women this was just what they longed to hear. Alexandra Kollontai had been the only prominent Bolshevik to applaud Lenin's first speech on returning to Russia. But soon he had the support of all the other leaders, and as exiled revolutionaries flocked back to Russia the Bolsheviks' following steadily increased.

Women in the Bolshevik party

Women, once introduced to the novelty and excitement of political activity, became some of the party's bravest and most radical members. A few months earlier they had stormed the streets of Petrograd; now they were opposing the Provisional Government and its vague promises of reform. With the help of the Bolsheviks, they organised demonstrations against rising prices and for an increase in their pensions. They needed higher pay, state-supported nurseries, maternity benefits and voting rights – and they needed the Bolsheviks to spell this out in their programme.

Most men in the Bolshevik party, and many women too – even passionate revolutionaries like Konkordia Samoilova, Nadezhda Krupskaya and Inessa Armand – still argued, despite the events of the past months, that women were too inexperienced and indisciplined to organise anything on their own. They still talked of women 'creating divisions' in the party. The Bolsheviks, now so popular and powerful, would do much more for women than women could do for themselves, they said.

But some women Bolsheviks disagreed. Alexandra Kollontai urged her women friends in the party leadership that every party organisation should have its own women's **bureau**, with one local member responsible for it. Her suggestion was rejected. She continued, nevertheless, to urge the party to appeal more boldly to women and listen to their needs.

It seems strange that Kollontai's women friends were so afraid of the idea of any sort of separate women's work. Most of them had worked on the Bolshevik women's paper, *Rabotnitsa*. Many of them were now among the Bolsheviks' most popular public speakers, too, and in their speeches they were especially anxious to present the Bolsheviks' message to women.

Kollontai was particularly popular. She was given the job of addressing sailors of the Helsingfors fleet. Sailing out on a cutter to the warships of the fleet, she would appeal to the sailors to support the Bolsheviks; despite some heckling and jeering, she was soon able to report back that the sailors would all be with the Bolsheviks. Her passionate speeches and elegant appearance did not go unnoticed by critical journalists, who indulged in their usual unpleasant methods of attack. There were hints of wardrobes full of clothes bought with 'German gold' – although in fact her trunk had been stolen on the way back to Russia, and she had only one dress. Other women speakers and organisers were victims of the same kind of innuendo.

Konkordia Samoilova had been a Bolshevik since 1902. She had worked in the underground movement for many years as

Alexandra Kollontai: an ardent activist for the Bolshevik and women's causes

31

'Comrade Natasha', and in 1913 had joined the *Pravda* editorial board as editor of the women's page. In 1914, as an editor of *Rabotnitsa*, she had been arrested and imprisoned. She was released in March 1917, and was now addressing meetings. Lyudmilla Stal had also been an editor of *Rabotnitsa*; now she was speaking to sailors of the Kronstadt fleet. Klavdia Nikolaeva had first joined the Bolsheviks as a young typesetter in 1908, and was now a full-time party-worker; she had helped to organise the laundresses' strike. Praskovia Kudelli had taught in workers' clubs in 1905, and was now running a school for women revolutionaries. Nadezhda Krupskaya, Anna Itkina and Zhenya Egorova, all long-standing Bolshevik members, were speaking to large crowds of women in the working-class districts of Narva and Vyborg.

Vera Slutskaya, secretary of the Vasilev Island Bolshevik committee, was also much loved by her women friends, who called her 'our iron Vera'. As a young Bolshevik in 1908 she had fiercely opposed Kollontai for

Nadezhda Krupskaya in the early years of Soviet power

attending feminist meetings and organising women's clubs, but by 1917 she was one of Kollontai's greatest allies. She had been a medical student until March, but had dropped her studies to work full-time for the Bolsheviks, and was now using her medical experience to train factory women as *sanitarki*. She was also in charge of political work amongst Petrograd's women. It was through talking to them that she realised that what was needed was a special women's bureau of the party, to which each district would send a woman representative. Despite grumbling from some men that the scheme 'reeked of feminism', Slutskaya's proposal was eventually approved: her position in the party and long membership had earned her the respect of her comrades.

Women Bolsheviks bring back *Rabotnitsa*

The old *Rabotnitsa* had been brought out under the Tsar. Its editors had been harassed by the police and imprisoned, and the paper had eventually been closed down. Now, for the first time in Russian history, revolutionary propaganda was legal, and the new *Rabotnitsa* stood at the centre of a growing Bolshevik propaganda network among women.

A *Rabotnitsa* school was set up, which trained factory women in the art of public speaking, then sent them back to the factories to teach others and distribute *Rabotnitsa*. Meanwhile the editors – Samoilova, Stal, Kollontai, Nikolaeva and others – would spend their days as before, talking to women and addressing meetings, then return late at night to the paper's offices to turn the day's experiences into articles.

The new *Rabotnitsa* first appeared on the streets of Russia's cities on 10 May 1917, as a weekly paper now, rather than monthly. It sold out immediately. Its print-run was increased from 40,000 to 50,000, and still it sold out. No one had anticipated just how popular it would be. But its popularity was well deserved, for its articles were always fresh, original and close to women's hearts.

Soon the editors started to organise massive *Rabotnitsa* rallies in Petrograd's circus buildings, and suddenly everyone was talking of *Rabotnitsa*. For hundreds of men and women these rallies provided some welcome light relief from the cares of the factory and the bread-queue. Hundreds of others heard the Bolsheviks speak for the first time, and were moved. 'Who hasn't seen Petrograd's circuses hasn't seen the revolution!' went the saying, as women crowded in to hear Kollontai or Samoilova recount the ways in which war had harmed women, and what the Bolsheviks proposed to do about it.

The July Days

By the summer of 1917 daily bread rations were down to half a pound per person. People were exhausted, desperate and starving. 'We lack the strength to live under these conditions', one leading trade unionist appealed to the government. On the railways and in the factories there was a wave of strikes that often developed into violent clashes with bosses and foremen. Demonstrations became massive; on some days as many as 50,000 of Petrograd's two million citizens thronged the streets until late at night, and the city was full of tension. 'PEACE, BREAD AND LAND!' read the banners, 'ALL POWER TO THE SOVIETS!', 'THE RIGHT TO LIFE IS HIGHER THAN THE RIGHT TO PRIVATE PROPERTY!' In the villages too,

tension rose, as returning soldiers joined peasants in looting and burning manor houses and seizing the land.

Anarchy ruled, the government was powerless. Russian troops continued to be sent to the front lines, and died in huge numbers. Five ministers resigned from the Provisional Government, fearing the revolution was imminent. Barricades went up in Petrograd.

On 3 July, 35,000 workers from the Putilov arms factory came out on strike. The machine-gun regiment joined them, with their guns, and asked other regiments to support them. Then the Red Guards appeared on the streets, supported by several armoured cars donated by the army and large numbers of women fighters, runners and *sanitarki*. Next they contacted workers and sailors at the garrisons of Kronstadt and Helsingfors, in the Gulf of Finland. On 4 July 20,000 sailors sailed into the capital to swell the demonstrations there. 'We want immediate confiscation of the land, and workers' control over industry!' they demanded. 'All power to the soviets!' Braving police snipers on the roofs and ignoring Lenin's advice to 'stay calm', the sailors then climbed through the windows of the Tauride Palace and demanded a meeting with the soviet leaders. They were eventually driven back by a

The July Days: tension rising in the streets of Petrograd, July 1917

Violence erupting at the beginning of the Bolshevik July uprising in Petrograd, 1917

battalion of soldiers still loyal to the government, and hundreds of Bolsheviks were arrested as 'German agents', out to sabotage a Russian victory.

The Bolshevik revolution

By September, 1917, the peasants' revolt was past the point of no return. Most soldiers were supporting the Bolsheviks, the railway and telegraph workers were openly sabotaging the Provisional Government and the workers were ready to fight. 'We stand on the threshold of world revolution!' said Lenin. The Bolsheviks were ready to take power.

To women Bolsheviks like Alexandra Kollontai, Konkordia Samoilova and Klavdia Nikolaeva, it seemed all the more urgent that women should have the chance to discuss what *they* wanted from the revolution. What was needed, they decided, was a congress – to take place *before* the revolution – at which women could get together and bring some of their problems into the open. The scheme was approved by the party, letters were sent to hundreds of women in the Petrograd area, and the congress was planned to open at the

Forward Club on Malaya Bolotnaya Street on 29 October.

But events moved faster than the organisers had anticipated. By early October the soldiers' demands that the Bolsheviks take power could no longer be delayed.

On 10 October the party leaders came out of hiding to hold a highly secret meeting at which they voted overwhelmingly that 'the armed uprising has fully and inevitably matured'. The insurrection was planned for 24 October, the opening day of the Second Congress of Soviets. A special bureau was formed under Trotsky's leadership to arm factory-workers, and soon every factory, warship and barracks in Russia was ready to take up arms for the Bolsheviks.

On 22 October – the 'Day of the Soviet' – there were huge demonstrations in the capital. The government locked themselves in the Winter Palace. The Red Guards came out on the streets with their guns; the red-kerchiefed *sanitarki* assembled, ready to tend the wounded; and the battleship *Aurora* sailed down the Neva River and aimed its guns at the Winter Palace; Bolshevik central committee members were summoned to the

34

Smolny Institute, once an Institute for girls of the nobility and now the headquarters of the Bolshevik revolution. The Bolshevik Red Guard was strengthened and extra bullets were made available.

Outside, young soldiers and *sanitarki* gathered nervously on the muddy cobbled streets alongside the Neva River. Inside, canteens were set up to feed the people, and the long corridors rang to the tramp of army boots as endless processions of soldiers reported to Leon Trotsky, in charge of the revolutionary forces.

The next day the Ministry of Religion, the telephone exchange and the State Bank were seized and occupied by soldiers. The government had now lost the support of all the major regiments, and the landed and wealthy were packing their bags to leave. The Winter Palace was guarded by soldiers and women of the famous **Women's Death Battalion**, who were loyal to the government. On 25 October a party of soldiers, sailors and *sanitarki* set off for the Winter Palace, and forcing their way past the soldiers guarding it they went in and arrested the cabinet. The Provisional Government was no more.

All that day delegates poured into the Smolny Institute, and that evening the building was packed with soldiers, peasants, sailors and working men and women. At 9.20 pm they heard muffled shots as the battleship *Aurora* fired blanks to signal the collapse of the Provisional Government. Lenin spoke then, to deafening applause. 'We shall now proceed to the construction of the socialist order', he announced, and then went on to read his 'peace declaration to the peoples of all warring countries'.

The Bolsheviks were in power now, and peace was no longer a dream. The rich and powerful in Russia, helped by the governments of the West, fought to defend their position and defeat the new government. But countless ordinary people were prepared to fight to the death to defend their revolution. For them, October 1917 was the start of a new era: an end to humiliation, hypocrisy and fear; the promise of peace, bread and land; and the birth of a new society in which men and women could live and work together as equals.

The storming of the Winter Palace in October 1917, from a painting by Kochergin

6

After 1917

The Western powers, ignoring the Bolsheviks' peace proposals, desperately wanted Russia to stay in the war against Germany, They also hoped against hope that the precarious new government would collapse. When it did not, they decided to give it a push. Invasion plans, drawn up in December 1917 by Britain and France, were approved by Japan and the United States. Over the next three years Russia was invaded by fourteen powers from almost every direction.

The Bolsheviks, poor and isolated, did not imagine they could last more than a few weeks without support from abroad, and clung desperately to their hopes of a world revolution. The 'White Guards', the tsarist generals helped by the mighty armies of the West, were confident of smashing the revolution in a few days. But they had not counted on people's resistance. The Red Army grew in strength and confidence, and over the next three years countless men and women would summon up their last drop of strength to defend the revolution.

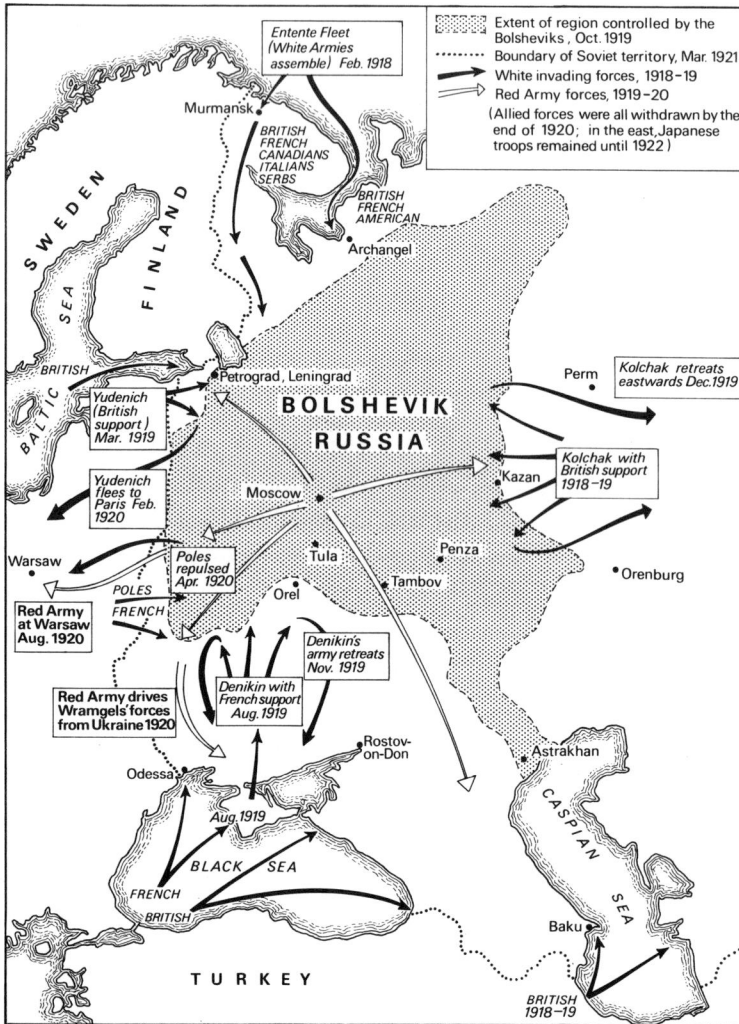

The Wars of Intervention, 1918–21

Lenin (in front of door) and others members of the new government – the 'Soviet of Peoples' Commissars'

Russians defend their revolution

On 29 October, when Cossacks loyal to the Provisional Government encircled Petrograd, thousands of men, women and children grabbed spades, shovels and whatever came to hand, and poured through the streets to the city gates. There they dug ditches, built barricades and barbed-wire fences and fought off the enemy. Petrograd was saved. Three days after taking power the Bolsheviks had scored their first victory.

The Bolsheviks gave people new hope; for millions the revolution was a time of tremendous optimism and energy. There was a great feast of meetings, in which soldiers, schoolchildren, housewives and even passengers on long train journeys took part. And the new government – the 'Soviet of Commissars' – passed ambitious decrees inspiring people all over Russia no longer to bow the head or take orders

But the Bolsheviks had inherited a ramshackle government that was terribly short of money. Many officials remained loyal to the old government and refused to co-operate, destroying papers, making off with funds and generally creating chaos. They spread wild and frightening rumours too. The Bolsheviks

wanted to nationalise women, they said, force twelve-year-old girls to marry, and snatch babies from their mothers in order to have them reared by the state. Such rumours were aimed particularly at women and played upon their deepest fears, and, however fantastic, many believed them. For despite the role women had taken on during the past few months of revolution, and despite all the Bolsheviks' promises of a better life for women, there were still many areas of women's lives that remained vulnerable. And now most women, drained by war and exhausted by lack of food, longed more than anything else for some peace of mind.

Women's lives after the revolution

As men were conscripted and killed, families were torn apart and more and more women lived alone with their children. Their lives were desperately hard. Many worked twelve or fourteen hours a day – and then had to do the housework. In those days housework involved hours of labour, particularly in a backward Russia, where drainage was inadequate and kitchens were primitive. Thousands of children were left to wander the streets while their mothers worked. Many women simply could

37

not support their children and left them in wretched orphanages. Some, unable to find work, were forced into prostitution.

Yet from this suffering women learned a quite extraordinary courage and strength, and for many women the revolution and the war that followed was a time of immense excitement and hope. Some 74,000 women, many of them still in their teens, joined the Red Army. There they learned to handle rifles, joined women's regiments and were gradually accepted into men's regiments, doing combat duty in times of siege and police work in times of lull. Gradually men and women learned to work together and to see each other as comrades. Not surprisingly, many women loved the freedom of working for the Bolsheviks in the early days of the revolution, and saw their experiences then as a model for things to come. The Bolsheviks now had to persuade women that they had their interests at heart.

Indeed one of the first laws passed by the new government, on 20 December 1917, was a new marriage decree. Men over eighteen and women over sixteen could now marry (provided they were not related); they could choose which surname to take afterwards; and women could sue for divorce and receive alimony. This law simplified marriage considerably. But mere laws could not automatically change men's age-old prejudices against women. Alexandra Kollontai, for one, realised this only too painfully: she was the victim of a great deal of gossip when she married a sailor, several years younger than herself.

Kollontai was the only woman in the government, the only person in that government able to speak for women. The Bolsheviks were too poor, and too accustomed to overlooking women, to do any more than make them men's equals in *law*, she said. It was women themselves who must fight for their full equality – by organising their own groups in the factories, unions and soviets, deciding what laws they needed to protect them, and then ensuring that these laws were worth more than the paper they were written on. If the Bolsheviks were seriously interested in liberating women they must first liberate them from housework, she said, by setting up

state-run canteens, nurseries and laundries. Only then could a woman be both a mother and a worker without one job taking away from the other. But it was women themselves who would first have to persuade men that this was worthy of their serious attention.

That was to have been the purpose of the women's congress she and her friends had planned before the revolution, but the congress had had to be delayed. Now letters were sent out again to women all over the Petrograd region, inviting one delegate for every 500 women to attend Petrograd's First House of Culture from 6 to 18 November.

The First Congress of Petrograd Working Women

As Konkordia Samoilova, Klavdia Nikolaeva and Alexandra Kollontai stood at the door to greet the women they soon realised they had underestimated how eager they would be to attend. They had expected about eighty, but in fact some five hundred arrived, and extra food and accommodation had to be provided.

Samoilova spoke first to welcome them; then Kollontai spoke. Look out for your own interests, she said, get the party to pass the laws you need at work, then make sure those laws are kept. All women, she went on, married or not, needed sixteen weeks' paid maternity leave, and must receive enough money to pay for a friend to take time off work too to help with the birth. Then they needed nurseries at the factories, warm rooms in which to feed their babies, and regular time off work to do so. Finally, they needed to be protected from long hours, night shifts and all work damaging to their health. Kollontai sat down to great applause.

The following month, the Bolsheviks turned many of these proposals into law.

Childcare

There was, however, an even more tragic and urgent problem that this law promised to deal with. Thousands of women, widowed or abandoned by their husbands and unable to support themselves, had been forced to leave

By 1917 thousands of orphans were left to fend for themselves

their children in miserable children's homes – known as 'angel factories'. These poor orphans would escape as soon as they were old enough, and by 1917 thousands of waifs were roaming the streets, hungry and often armed, managing to exist only by stealing food or prostituting themselves. Some went to school just to be fed, but many teachers were opposed to the new government, so food was often not provided for them there.

The first thing the new law aimed to do was to ensure that women were kept healthy and not overworked, so they could feed their babies properly and not abandon them in the first place. Next, the old 'angel factories' were to be abolished, and modern children's homes set up in their place. The Nikolaev Institute, a dilapidated old 'angel factory' on the Moika Canal, was to be abolished and replaced by a modern maternity home, a 'Palace for Mothers and Babies'. This was to be a model for other mother and baby homes in Russia, and the first real practical proof that the Bolsheviks took women's needs seriously.

The countess running the old Institute was moved into a side wing, while Alexandra Kollontai and her team of assistants cleaned and painted the building, put up curtains, moved in beds and cots and set up a nursery, a medical laboratory, a dairy and a library. They put up illustrated posters on baby care

and child development. 'SHARE YOUR MILK WITH OTHER MOTHERS!' these read, and 'BE A MOTHER NOT JUST TO YOUR OWN CHILD BUT TO ALL CHILDREN!' By the end of January 1918, hundreds of pregnant women had eagerly applied to have their babies there.

But other women were not so happy about these changes and were only too ready to listen to the countess. The heathen Bolsheviks had taken down the icons (= sacred pictures), she said; the nurses were sluts who let sailors stay the night with them. When the building went up in flames just a few hours before it was due to open, there was little doubt as to who had caused it.

Civil war

However, the Bolsheviks were suffering far worse things at the hands of their enemies abroad.

In March 1918 the Germans, confident of forcing the revolution to collapse, made the Bolsheviks sign a peace treaty at Brest-Litovsk. Lenin, who wanted peace at any price for the exhausted Russian people, persuaded his government to accept the Germans' punishing demands: having lost millions of her people in the war, Russia was now to repay her aggressor with over a third of her population, most of her coalfields, about half her industrial towns and factories and a third of her farming land.

But even as this treaty was being signed, Germany, France, the USA and Japan were launching a massive attack on their Bolshevik enemies, while Britain was landing troops at Murmansk and Archangel. Supported by the tsarist admirals and generals (the 'White Guards'), and backed by vast amounts of money and equipment, these anti-Bolshevik troops made up a vast and highly trained force bent on putting down the revolution.

In Russia, the government was evacuated from Petrograd to the Kremlin fortress in Moscow, industry was put on a war footing, all Bolshevik speakers were summoned to the war fronts, and millions of Russians, many of them women, joined the Red Army to beat off the invaders.

Anti-tsarist propaganda on an agit-prop train

Women fighters and women at home

Many women went off to the war fronts, where they took to the highly dangerous tasks of guerilla warfare. Many others infiltrated the enemy camps as spies. But it was as public speakers that they were most valued, and it was a woman named Varya Kasparova who trained men and women in Moscow to travel to the war areas and inspire the exhausted people there to defend the revolution.

Alexandra Kollontai travelled thousands of miles on a special train equipped with slide-shows, medical supplies, films and theatre groups. Stopping at the small villages and towns she came to, she would speak to the terrified and exhausted people and urge them to stay on and fight the Whites. Konkordia Samoilova was another very popular speaker. Travelling up and down the Volga River on the *Red Star* steamer, she would persuade the women she met to support the Red Army by making bandages, nursing soldiers and doing volunteer defence work.

But what of the great majority of women they met? Women whose husbands had died or deserted them still had a desperately hard struggle to support themselves and their children. The shops were empty, food was scarce, and meals consisted of little more than thin soup, barley gruel, tiny pieces of dried fish and slivers of bread. Most of them lived in dirty crowded flats, usually sharing lavatories and kitchens with several other families. Scarce food made for constant bickering and pilfering.

Yet the Bolshevik government, beset by war and poverty, had little time for women's problems.

The revolution has brought rights for women on paper, but in fact it has made life much harder for them. *Alexandra Kollontai*

What women needed was practical help, not just promises.

Opening a nursery for working women's children attracts far more women to us than ten speeches. *Konkordia Samoilova*

The Women's Commission: All-Russian Congress of Women for 1918

When Samoilova and Kollontai returned to Moscow from their travels the first thing they did was to ask the Bolshevik Central Committee to set up a special women's commission to tackle some of these problems. The men were shocked. 'What, are there to be two parties now, one for men and one for women?' But eventually they relented a little and allowed them to organise a women's congress in November, at which women could air some of their complaints.

When we applied for accommodation for a hundred women we were told: 'Don't bother, it's not worth it, you'll never get that many.'
Alexandra Kollontai

In fact over a thousand women came, most of them peasants. They came from all parts of Russia too, many making long and difficult journeys across war zones, and arriving exhausted and hungry. The organisers applied to the Central Committee for extra food and accommodation, and were eventually allowed to use the Grand Hall of Unions in the Kremlin – after the women had threatened to riot and occupy it.

The women, in their sheepskin coats, red headscarfs and felt boots, settled back comfortably in the plush seats, and the congress opened with cheering and shouting. Inessa Armand spoke first, starting with a rousing attack on pots and pans and housework and ending with a call for more state-run canteens and nurseries. This was met with some anxious cries of 'We will not give up our children!' Alexandra Kollontai stood up then, to much cheering, and assured them that the Bolsheviks had no such intention. The whole point of setting up canteens and nurseries was to set women free from endless household chores, and give them more time for the more enjoyable things of life – such as reading, seeing friends and going to concerts and meetings. More importantly, nurseries would free working women from endless anxieties about their children, and allow them to enjoy their time with them. And canteens and laundries would allow them to spend more time with their husbands. Only then, she said, would men and women be able to live together happily, unselfishly and as equals, without jealousy or resentment. Kollontai was warmly applauded, and the proceedings ended with the singing of *Internationale*, the Socialist anthem.

The congress was such a success that the government finally agreed that every factory and village should elect women delegates for a three-month period. These delegates would find out what women wanted, inform their

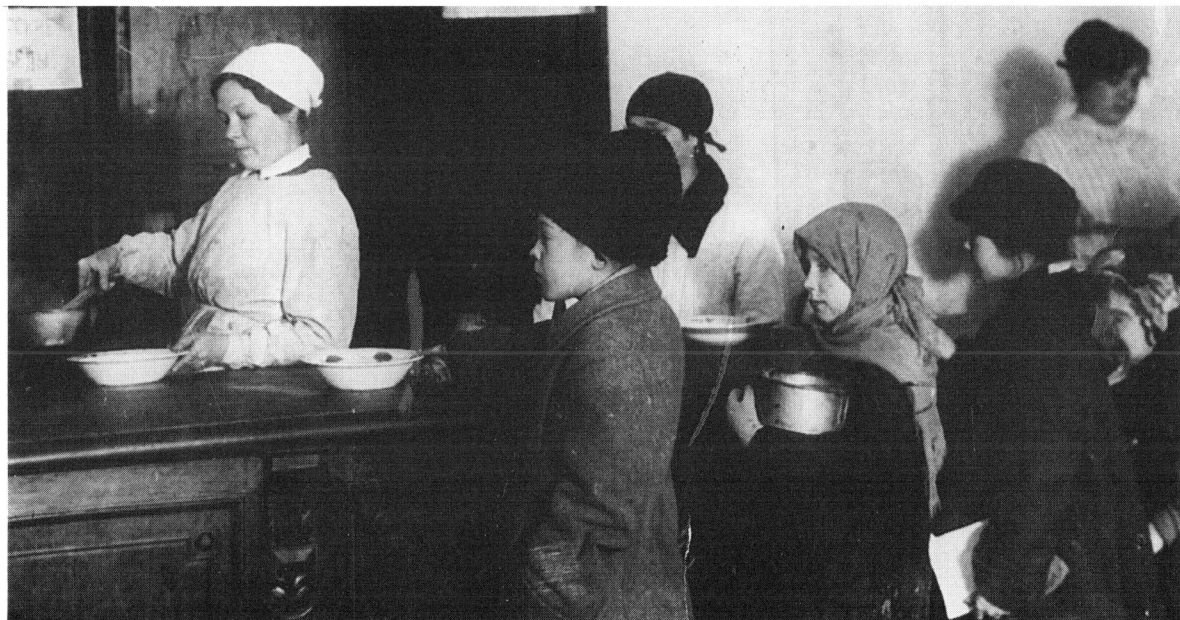

Children being fed at a school during the severe food shortage in Petrograd, 1918

local parties, and report back to a central Women's Commission, based in Moscow and headed by Alexandra Kollontai, Inessa Armand and a Bolshevik party worker called Vera Moirova. The woman delegate, in her red headscarf and shabby clothes, was soon a familiar and popular figure in every town and village, trudging from house to house, often taking abandoned children into her own home, and when need be taking up a rifle and going off to fight.

One of the Commission's most urgent jobs was to set up more homes for children orphaned in the war – particularly in the Crimea and the Ukraine, where fighting was heaviest. Next, as the prospect of another starving winter threatened, the Commission worked with local soviets in organising canteens in towns and villages. The Central Committee agreed to supply these canteens with extra provisions, and the Commission had no trouble in persuading women that they would be better off eating there than trying to cook at home. Soon most people in Moscow and Petrograd were queuing up for plates of porridge, strips of horsemeat, slabs of margarine and glasses of tea. Although food supplies at these canteens were in fact quite good, the food was abominably cooked, and there was much grumbling in the food queues. But it was a start, however rough and ready.

Few people in the government, however, saw the need to provide women with anything more than this sort of emergency relief. The Bolsheviks were fighting for the survival of their government, and most men in the party still refused to take women's grievances seriously. They said women's problems could not be properly tackled until the end of the war.

By 1919 vast areas of Russia had fallen to the Whites (see map on p. 36). The British had set up governments in Archangel and Estonia. The French fleet was in the Black Sea. The Red Army was scourged by typhus, cholera and hunger. Millions of Russians had been killed by war, epidemic and famine – and still there was no prospect of peace.

Yet despite extreme suffering, the Bolsheviks won. Most peasants refused to support and feed the Whites, and one by one Bolshevik

42

defeats were turned into victories. In October 1920 the Whites finally withdrew, and the civil war came to an end.

But having defeated their enemies, the Bolsheviks now faced isolation and poverty. The foreign intervention and civil war had brought misery and disorganisation. People were deprived of fuel and existing on half-rations. Workers had been killed. Industry had ground to a halt. As Red Army soldiers returned to the towns and demanded work, women were usually the first to lose their jobs. Now unemployed, the women risked losing everything they had gained from the revolution, and being forced back into their previous enslavement.

These problems had always existed, even throughout the civil war. Yet whenever the Women's Commission tried to bring these problems to the party's attention, they were continually blocked by men's contemptuous attitudes to their work. There was such a flood of complaints from women all over Russia that the party was eventually forced to do something about it, and in September 1919 the Commission was raised to the status of a party department, led in Moscow by Inessa Armand.

The Zhenotdel

Women had played a heroic part in the Bolsheviks' victory. Everyone recognised that. The new Women's Department (or Zhenotdel) now had to persuade the government to consider women's needs after victory. The first thing they did was to organise women's conferences all over Russia, where women got together to discuss some of the ways they had suffered from the war. As men moved to other towns to serve in the army or work in the factories, they often left their wives and children for good and formed new ties. Most were too poor to give their wives alimony, and most had no desire to change their old irresponsible ways anyway. Countless women had been widowed too. For many of these women, alone and unable to find work, there was only one place to make a pitiful living for themselves and their children – on the streets. The economic crisis threatened to make the problem even worse.

1920, Great Famine. Over seven million Russian people died from the combined results of war, famine and epidemics

The Zhenotdel announced that any women found soliciting would be helped to find jobs and given medical attention. Only if they were found soliciting repeatedly would they be punished.

Another painful result of the war was a drastic increase in the number of unwanted pregnancies. Abortion was regarded as a dangerous operation, and was illegal. Yet countless women, desperate to avoid bearing children they could not support, had been forced to have illegal abortions – many of them dying or suffering serious complications as a result. The Zhenotdel, together with some progressive doctors and health workers, finally persuaded the government to legalise abortion (as a 'temporary health measure'), and in November 1920 Russia became the first country in the world to give women the right to free abortions in state hospitals.

Next, the Zhenotdel tackled women's problems at work. To make sure that the factories observed the new laws protecting women, every group of factory inspectors was to include at least one woman, who would see that women were protected from night-work and overtime, and given time off to feed their babies. More importantly, at a time when so many women were being forced out of work, the party must give them extra training to allow them to take the more skilled jobs. A lot of men in the unions disliked the idea of women competing with them for work in these times of rising unemployment. It was up to the party, said the Zhenotdel, to attack this sort of prejudice.

It was clear that women would have to begin to play their part in the government if their voices were to be heard. So the Zhenotdel organised a series of meetings in every town and village of Russia, where women were elected to work for three months in a local government department. There they could learn how the government worked and how to make it work best for women. After three months some women moved to a permanent government job, while others returned to their old life, where they shared their experiences with their friends. Many men could not accept this idea. 'If they take my wife away from me I cannot work!' shouted one man at a meeting.

Women were facing problems with the government too. Staff and funds were severely cut, so that by 1921, of 43 women originally working at the Zhenotdel headquarters, only

Moscow, 1920. Meeting of the Women of the East, organised by Alexandra Kollontai

23 remained. More and more local women's departments were illegally disbanded by regional parties. Zhenotdel organisers in Moscow protested in vain, finding that they were expected to sit through endlessly long meetings at which women's issues were invariably placed last on the agenda. When they objected they were told to sit outside until the discussion came round to women. Josef Stalin and his associates had a particularly hostile attitude to women, while most men in the government, according to Konkordia Samoilova, tended to dismiss women's work as 'beneath their dignity'.

The collapse of the Zhenotdel

In 1922 Lenin had a stroke which left him paralysed, and under Stalin, the new party secretary, the Zhenotdel suffered further cuts in funds and staff. Alexandra Kollontai, who in 1920 had replaced Inessa Armand as director of the Zhenotdel, was sacked for 'incompetence', and her writings and speeches on love and family life were attacked as 'scandalous'. Her place was taken by Sofia Smidovich whose status in the party was not high, and who had far more modest ambitions for women. More local women's departments were disbanded, and fewer women attended party congresses. It became much harder for the Zhenotdel to enforce equal pay for equal work, and to set up badly needed nurseries, canteens and laundries.

The Zhenotdel's success had been impressive. But it had always served the interests of the party and its leaders – who were all men. In 1930, when the government announced that the Zhenotdel was to be dissolved, there was very little opposition.

What did the revolution do for women?

The Bolshevik revolution had managed in a few short years to bring quite astounding changes to women's lives. The old form of family life was dead and buried now, and the

44

The Soviet woman of today: welder Nadezhda Chechneva

Bolsheviks pledged themselves to put something better in its place. The 1917 marriage law simplified marriage and divorce, and abortion was made legal. In 1926, a new Family Code removed even more restrictions on divorce and recognised all marriages, whether officially registered or not.

But despite all these progressive laws, the changing of family life was a deeply painful process, especially for women, and the government never did enough to ensure that the new society worked in their interests. Women's new confidence and energy was continually being obstructed by men determined to hold on to their old powers; politics remained largely a man's world.

In the severe climate of the late 1920s, when Soviet Russia geared itself up for its immense industrialisation programme, and in the three decades that followed, people were imprisoned and killed on the slightest suspicion of working against the government. Differences of opinion were banned and censored, women were silenced.

From 1918 to 1920, women had fought in the civil war. From 1928 to 1937, they were mobilised in vast numbers to carry out the programme of industrialisation of the First and Second Five-Year Plans. From 1941 to 1944, when the Soviet Union was invaded by the Nazis, women played a heroic part in that terrible war, and in Hitler's defeat.

Yet despite the extraordinary changes in women's lives, and the break-up of the old family life, many of the old attitudes to women still survived. Women whose husbands had died or left them during the civil war had a desperately hard struggle to support themselves and their children. Those who followed them in the succeeding generation continued to have their energy and health undermined by the daily exhaustion of the 'double burden' of having to earn money and be responsible for the housework and children.

Many women, however, were simply not prepared to give up what they had gained. The revolution had opened up new possibilities and had shown a way, however difficult, for women to be both workers and mothers. Women in the Soviet Union are still fighting these struggles today.

War and revolution created a new kind of woman, strong and independent, and in the Soviet Union today people still talk about women's extraordinary courage in those years and in the years that followed.

45

QUESTIONS

1 Read the petition presented to the Tsar in 1905 (page 16). Imagine you were one of the demonstrators and complete the petition.

2 A group of Russian women students in Zurich in the 1870s proposed setting up a study group for women only. Sofia Bardina, one of the organisers, said: 'At meetings with men, women usually keep quiet; we feel shy and so we don't say anything. But maybe with practice we'll learn to develop our thoughts logically, and then won't be afraid to speak in public. A women's circle would be a place where we could learn.'

   Vera Figner, another student, agreed but, according to her, many other women 'found it ridiculous that women should be afraid in the presence of men, and thought it would be much more natural and expedient to form a joint self-education circle without fear of masculine competition'.

   Imagine an argument between these two points of view using the additional knowledge you have gained from reading this book.

3 Identify the different sources in this book and say which you have found the most informative and why.

4 Find two other books on this topic and consider the following:
   (a) Which groups of people according to your two sources and this book were involved in the revolution? Do your sources differ? If so, how?
   (b) How can you explain the fact that people writing about the same event give such different impressions?
   (c) Supposing that your different sources give a very different impression of the immediate causes of the revolution, does this mean that one or other is useless as historical evidence, or could all be useful? Give reasons for your answers.
   (d) How could an historian check the reliability of these sources?
   (e) Put the publication dates of your sources in order. Can you learn anything about the authors' interpretation from this?
   (f) Which of your sources is
        – the least and most informative about the role of women?
        – the least and most sympathetic about the role of women?

5 In 1919, Lenin said: 'In the course of two years of Soviet power in one of the most backward countries of Europe, more has been done to emancipate woman, to make her the equal of the "strong sex", than has been done during the past 130 years by all the advanced, enlightened "democratic" republics of the world taken together.'

   Yet Alexandra Kollontai was saying, in 1918: 'The revolution has brought rights for women on paper, but in fact it has made life much harder for them.'

   In what ways had women's position changed and in what ways had it remained the same by 1918?

GLOSSARY

assassination sudden or surprise murder; refers in this book to the political, 'revenge' killing of important members of government by members of the People's Will Party, the Socialist Revolutionary Party etc.

autocracy supreme power in the hands of one person. It was Ivan the Terrible, in the sixteenth century, who first called himself 'autocrat', and his reign gave new autocratic powers to the rulers of Russia who followed him

babi bunty literally 'peasant women's riots'. In 1904, while their menfolk were away fighting in the Russo–Japanese War, peasant women looted and burnt the estates

Bolsheviks and **Mensheviks** differing attitudes emerged within the Russian Social Democratic Labour Party (*see below*), and these differences, however unimportant they may seem to us now, involved major disagreements about how to organise the revolution in Russia. They emerged into two separate groups (or 'factions') in 1903, at the Second Party Congress. The Bolsheviks (from Russian *bolshe*, 'more'), who claimed to be in the majority, believed, with Lenin, that the revolutionary party must be made up of a small number of 'professional revolutionaries'. The Mensheviks (from Russian *menshe*, 'less') wanted a party made up of the largest possible number of sympathisers. Although there were several attempts to patch up the rift, the two factions continued to go their separate ways, and after the Bolsheviks seized power in 1917 the Mensheviks declined to collaborate with the new government

bureau (as in women's bureau)   an office attached to local Bolshevik party organisations

Cossacks   (literally 'free warriors') – people living in the South of European Russia, southern Siberia and the Far East, In the eighteenth and nineteenth centuries prosperous new Cossack communities were set up by the government, the men being expected in return to serve in special Cossack military units. In the nineteenth and twentieth centuries Cossacks were frequently used for police purposes, and they gained a reputation for great cruelty

despotism   unlimited or uncontrolled authority

Duma   House of Representatives set up by Tsar Nicholas II after the 1905 revolution

emancipation   freedom from slavery or subjection. In Russia, 'the emancipation' meant first and foremost the emancipation of the serfs by Tsar Alexander II in 1861

International   First International, the International Workingman's Association, founded in London in 1864 to encourage co-operation between trade union movements in different countries. Second International (the Socialist International), founded in Paris in 1889 to unite the socialist parties of Europe (the largest and most important of which was the German Social Democratic Party). The Russian socialists attended the first congress and subsequent ones, although no single group within all the Russian socialist groups could be said to represent Russia

manifesto   a public declaration usually by a monarch or government, as in Tsar Nicholas II's Manifesto of 1905 promising the 'four freedoms'

Marxist   one who accepts the ideas of the German philosopher Karl Marx (1818–83), whose *Das Kapital* was a detailed account of working conditions in England. His conclusion, that the time was ripe for workers to seize power and make a revolution, was enthusiastically taken up by many Russians in the 1890s

Mensheviks   *see Bolsheviks*

nihilists   term used by conservatives in Russia in the 1850s, 60s and 70s to mean anyone who opposed the existing order. Used by nihilists themselves (or 'new people' as many preferred to be called) to mean those who rejected all the old relationships – between lords and peasants, factory-owners and workers, men and women – in order to live their lives in a more equal way

nationalism   devotion to one's own nation

piece-rates   pay that is measured by the quantity of work done, rather than by the time spent doing it

populists   from Latin *populus*, 'the people' – in nineteenth-century Russia, those who believed that the peasants would bring about a revolution, and that they provided the model for the society that would follow it

propaganda   ideas and theories spread and explained to people with the intention of making them firmly held convictions. **Propagandists** – those who devote themselves to spreading propaganda

Provisional Government   brought into being, as a temporary measure, by the abdication in March 1917, of Tsar Nicholas II

radicals   people who believe in fundamental social and political reforms

religious orthodoxy   strict adherence to the laws of the Russian Orthodox Church

Russian Orthodox Church   the main religious community in Russia, headed by the Patriarch of Moscow and All Russia

Russian Social Democratic Labour Party (RSDRP)   the first party of Marxist revolutionaries in Russia. Founded in 1898 at its first congress in Minsk. Split into Bolshevik and Menshevik factions at its second congress in 1903 (held in Brussels and London because it was an illegal party in Russia). In 1918 the Bolshevik faction of the RSDRP renamed itself the Russian Communist Party (Bolshevik)

St Petersburg   immediately after the outbreak of the First World War in August 1914 the official name of the Russian capital was changed from the German St Petersburg to the Russian Petrograd

serfs   peasants (80 per cent of the population) who were the hereditary property of a landowning master, and compelled to work on his land. In Russia, the growth of the landowning gentry throughout the fourteenth and fifteenth centuries meant that more and more land and peasants fell into their hands. Overtaxed and overworked,

Russian peasants gradually drifted into a slavery, long before the legal code of 1649 made serfdom a state institution. The serfs were freed in 1861

Tsar   sometimes spelt 'Czar', derives from the Latin *Caesar* (compare the German *Kaiser*) title of the rulers of Russia ever since Ivan the Terrible proclaimed himself Tsar in the sixteenth century

Women's Death Battalion   also known as Women's Shock Battalion – in May 1917 the Provisional Government, with the support of the Feminist League of Equality, organised special battalions of women (most of them young peasants) to fight at the front and inspire soldiers to fight the enemy to the death. In October 1917 members of the Women's Death Battalion guarded the Winter Palace, where the government had locked themselves in against the Bolsheviks

women's liberation   in various periods throughout the past two hundred years, and in various different countries, women have struggled to free themselves from positions of social and economic inequality. In Russia, such movements for women's liberation were seen in the 1860s, in 1905, and in the period roughly between the beginning of the First World War (1914) and the end of the Civil War (1920)

SOURCES QUOTED

Vera Karelina, 'Rabotnitsa v Gaponovskiich obshchestvakh' ('Working woman in the Gapon organisations'), in P. F. Kudelli (ed.), *Rabotnitsa v 1905 god v S. Peterburge* (*Working woman in 1905 in St Petersburg*), Leningrad, 1926

Alexandra Kollontai, *K istorii dvizhenia rabotnits v Rossii* (*Toward a history of the working women's movement in Russia*), Kharkov, 1920

Alexandra Kornilova-Moroz, 'Perovskaya i osnovanie kruzhka Chaikovtsev' ('Perovskaya and the founding of the Chaikovsky circle'), *Katorga i ssylka* (*Hard Labour and Exile*), no. 22, 1926

A contemporary factory report quoted in A. Ryazanova, *Zhenskii trud* (*Women's labour*), Moscow, 1924

Nadezhda Khvoshchina, quoted by V. I. Semyovskii in 'N. D. Khvoshchina-Zaionchovskaya', *Russkaya mysl* (*Russian Thought*), no. 10, 1890

V. Nekrasova, *Zhenskie vrachebnie kursy* (*Women's medical courses*)

Nekrasova in Elena Likhachova, *Materialy dlya istorii zhenskogo obrazovanii v Rossii* (Material for a History of Women's Education in Russia), St Petersburg, 1899–1901

E. A. Slovtsova-Kamskaya, 'Zhenshchina v seme i obshchestve' ('Women in the family and society'), *Istoricheskii vestnik* (*Historical Herald*), August 1881

Leon Trotsky, *History of the Russian Revolution*, translated by Max Eastman, New York, 1932

FURTHER READING

J. F. Aylett, *Russia in Revolution* (Links Series), Arnold, 1981

Marie Brown, *Russia and Revolution*, Blackie, 1979

David Footman, *Russian Revolutionaries*, Faber, 1962

L. Hartley, *The Russian Revolution*, Evans, 1980

Joan Hasler, *The Making of Russia*, Longmans, 1969

John Kennet, *The Growth of Modern Russia*, Blackie, 1967

David Killingray, *The Russian Revolution*, Harrap World History Programme, 1975

Peter Lane, *The USSR in the Twentieth Century*, Batsford, 1978

Ian Lister, *The Cold War*, Methuen, 1974

Martin McCauley, *The Stalin File*, Batsford, 1979

Fred Newman, *Leaders of the Russian Revolution*, Wayland Publishers Ltd, 1981

Sally Pickering, *Twentieth-century Russia*, Oxford University Press, 1965

J. Quinn, *The Russian Revolution*, University Tutorial Press, 1972

John Robottom, *Modern Times: Modern Russia*, Longmans 1969

D. M. Sturley, *World in Transformation: Russia*, Ginn and Co, 1969

Stephen White, *USSR. Portrait of a Superpower*, Blackie, 1978

S. H. Wood, *Russia in the Early Twentieth Century (1904–24)*, James Brodie Ltd, 1966